The Latin American Drug Trade

Scope, Dimensions, Impact, and Response

T0162210

Peter Chalk

Prepared for the United States Air Force

 PROJECT AIR FORCE

The research described in this report was sponsored by the United States Air Force under Contract FA7014-06-C-0001. Further information may be obtained from the Strategic Planning Division, Directorate of Plans, Hq USAF.

Library of Congress Control Number: 2011927970

ISBN 978-0-8330-5179-0

Published 2011 by the RAND Corporation
1776 Main Street, P.O. Box 2138, Santa Monica, CA 90407-2138
1200 South Hayes Street, Arlington, VA 22202-5050
4570 Fifth Avenue, Suite 600, Pittsburgh, PA 15213-2665
RAND URL: http://www.rand.org/
To order RAND documents or to obtain additional information, contact
Distribution Services: Telephone: (310) 451-7002;
Fax: (310) 451-6915; Email: order@rand.org

Preface

Transnational crime remains a particularly serious problem in Latin America, affecting numerous states both in and beyond the region and having severe repercussions for political, economic, and human security. Although a range of issues confront policymakers and decision-makers, most are, in some way or another, connected with the drug trade. This monograph examines the scope and dimensions of cocaine and heroin production emanating from Latin America; the main methods and routes that are used to ship narcotics between source, transit, and consumption countries; and the principal consequences that are associated with this particular manifestation of transnational crime.

This monograph is based on research conducted during fiscal years 2009 and 2010 as part of a study, "U.S. Security Roles in Latin America," that identified and analyzed the major security trends in Latin America and the implications of regional developments for the stability of friendly states and broader U.S. interests.

The research reported here was sponsored by the Deputy Director for Operational Planning, Policy and Strategy, Office of the Deputy Chief of Staff for Operations, Plans and Requirements, Headquarters U.S. Air Force (HQ USAF/A5X), and conducted within the Strategy and Doctrine Program of RAND Project AIR FORCE.

RAND Project AIR FORCE

RAND Project AIR FORCE (PAF), a division of the RAND Corporation, is the U.S. Air Force's federally funded research and development center for studies and analyses. PAF provides the Air Force with independent analyses of policy alternatives affecting the development, employment, combat readiness, and support of current and future aerospace forces. Research is conducted in four programs: Force Modernization and Employment; Manpower, Personnel, and Training; Resource Management; and Strategy and Doctrine.

Additional information about PAF is available on our website: http://www.rand.org/paf/

Contents

Figures

Tables

Summary

Drug Production and Trafficking

Colombia currently accounts for the vast bulk of cocaine produced in Latin America. In 2009, the country produced 270 metric tons (MT) of cocaine, making it the principal supplier for both the United States and the worldwide market. Besides Colombia, Peru and Bolivia constitute two additional important sources of cocaine in Latin America. In 2009, these two countries generated enough base material to respectively yield 225 and 195 MT of refined product.

Between 60 and 65 percent of all Latin American cocaine is trafficked to the United States, the bulk of which is smuggled via the eastern Pacific/Central American corridor. The remainder is sent through the Caribbean island chain, with the Dominican Republic, Puerto Rico, and Haiti acting as the main transshipment hubs. In both cases, Mexico serves as the main point of entry to mainland America, presently accounting for the vast majority of all illicit drug imports to the United States.

Increasing amounts of Latin American cocaine are now also being sent to Europe, reflecting higher street prices than those in the United States and shifting consumer demand patterns toward this particular narcotic (and derivates, such as crack). The majority of the Colombian cocaine that is trafficked to Europe, either directly or via West Africa, is exported from Venezuela.

In addition to cocaine, Colombia also represents a relatively important source for North America opiates, historically accounting for around half of the white heroin consumed east of the Mississippi.

Although there has been a marked decline in opium-production levels in the past several years—largely due to successful poppy-eradication efforts—shipments still take place, with the main trafficking route running up the eastern Pacific to Mexico.

Main Players

The Revolutionary Armed Forces of Colombia (Fuerzas Armadas Revolucionarias de Colombia, or FARC) currently represents the principal narco-player in Colombia. The organization is involved in all aspects of the drug trade, from production through refining to trafficking, and is thought to earn anywhere between US$200 million and US$300 million per year from these activities (which is thought to equate to roughly half of its overall operational budget). Historically, most of this income was used to underwrite and sustain FARC's insurgent war against the Bogotá government. In recent years, however, it appears that elements in the organization have increasingly turned to narcotics as an exclusive economic endeavor, with greed and profit rather than politics and ideology being the main motivational drivers.

Reemerging paramilitaries, euphemistically referred to as *bandas criminales emergentes* (criminal groups, or simply BACRIM), also play a prominent role in the drug trade. Colombian authorities have identified 11 main gangs (down from 33–67 between 2006 and 2007), four of which remain at the forefront of national security concern: the Don Mario Gang, Ejército Revolucionario Popular Anticomunista (Erpac), the Rastrojos, and Los Paisas.

A third player on the Colombian drug scene is the Norte del Valle (NDV) cartel, which, during the 1990s, was the country's most-powerful narcotics crime group. The cartel has progressively diminished in prominence, however, due to growing factionalism in its ranks and the capture or elimination of some of its leading personalities, including the NDV supreme "godfather" and one of the most-wanted men in Colombia, Diego Montoya (a.k.a. Don Diego).

Finally, there are indications that the National Liberation Army (Ejército de Liberación Nacional, or ELN) is becoming more-intimately involved in cocaine production and trafficking. According to U.S. and Colombian officials, the group is increasingly reorienting its traditional focus on fundraising away from extortion and kidnapping toward the far more-lucrative drug trade—with much of this activity concentrated along the northern Pacific coast.

In Peru and Bolivia, the drug trade is largely dispersed among a plethora of amorphous, nonspecific groups. These indigenous entities generally confine their focus to the cultivation of local fields, with actual processing and refining taking place in Brazil and, to a lesser extent, Argentina. Colombian and Mexican groups appear to dominate the latter effort, developing it as an integral component of their overall transatlantic narcotics export chain.

Apart from FARC, the Autodefensas Unidas de Colombia (AUC), the ELN, and smaller Peruvian and Bolivian cartels, organizations in Mexico constitute a critical component in the overall Latin American drug trade. These groups dominate control of the actual movement of narcotics into the mainland United States, as well as subsequent distribution in major metropolitan areas. According to a 2008 assessment prepared by the U.S. Department of Justice, Mexican trafficking organizations have gained more control over the supply of drugs to the United States than any other ethnic criminal group (availed by the large expatriate community that exists across the country), yielding revenue levels that are thought to be in the billions of dollars.

Seven Mexican syndicates have remained at the forefront of the trade: the Gulf cartel, La Familia, Los Zetas, the Beltrán Leyva organization, the Sinaloa cartel, the Carrillo Fuentes syndicate (a.k.a. the Juarez cartel), and the Arellano Félix organization (a.k.a. the Tijuana cartel). These groups can be divided into two main, competing blocs that essentially pitch the Sinaloa cartel, the Gulf cartel, and La Familia—which collectively formed the New Federation in February 2010—against a loose pattern of shifting alliances among the remaining five organizations.

Beyond Central and Latin America, two other major entities play an important role in the trafficking of Andean cocaine. First are West African syndicates, particularly those based in Ghana and Guinea-Bissau. These groups constitute the main vehicle by which Colombian, Peruvian, and Bolivian cocaine is (indirectly) shipped to Western Europe. Second is the Calabrian 'Ndrangheta, a principal mafia in Italy and the one with the greatest international reach. The group is thought to be capable of purchasing and moving up to three tons of Colombian cocaine at a time—with a wholesale price of roughly €60 million (approximately US$74.5 million).

Trafficking Vessels

More than 80 percent of Latin American cocaine that is trafficked to the United States, either directly or via Mexico, arrives by means of noncommercial maritime conveyance. Up until 2006, most Latin American cocaine and heroin was moved nonstop to Mexico in single consignments. Deepwater fishing trawlers were the favored vessels for these shipments due to their sophisticated navigation and communication technologies.

Although fishing trawlers are still periodically used for drug runs, Latin American syndicates have progressively moved away from shipping large volumes via direct routes due to more-effective interdiction in the eastern Pacific. The preferred method today is to spread risk by smuggling smaller but more-numerous volumes in "go-fasts." These vessels have a top speed of around 70 mph and are capable of moving up to 2 MT of drugs at a time.

Apart from surface boats, Colombian syndicates also use semisubmersibles. These vessels are principally employed for large drug runs in the eastern Pacific and can carry loads of between 6 and 10 MT. The standard range for a semi is between 500 and 1,000 nautical miles (nm). However, some have been purpose-built to reach distances upward of 1,500 nm, which puts them well within the vicinity of Mexican waters.

Impact

The drug trade has had an effect across South, Central, and North America. In Colombia, revenue from the production and trafficking of heroin and cocaine has provided FARC with sufficient operational capital to maintain an active war footing in its ongoing conflict against Bogotá. Compounding the situation in Colombia are the activities of reemerging paramilitaries, whose fighting and competition have contributed to an increasingly serious humanitarian crisis.

Further afield, the cocaine trade is feeding a growing addiction problem. Indeed, countries, such as Puerto Rico and the Dominican Republic, have experienced so massive an increase in drug use that they are now effectively as much consumption states as transit hubs.

In the United States, the sale, distribution, and use of narcotics has contributed to addiction and public health problems, further exacerbated the breakdown of social and family relations, and fueled street violence in prominent end-user cities. It has also significantly impeded fiscal growth and stability by diverting scarce resources away from more-productive uses and negatively interacted with other transborder concerns, such as weapon trafficking, people smuggling, and the migration of Central American gang violence.

It is in Mexico, however, that the pernicious societal impact of the Latin American cocaine and heroin trade has been greatest. In particular, it has contributed to what amounts to the wholesale breakdown of basic civility across the country, something that has been particularly evident in the northern border states. Apart from fostering extreme violence, the narcotics trade has also decisively undermined political stability by feeding pervasive corruption throughout the police and administrative bureaucracy.

U.S. Responses

In moving to mitigate the Latin American cocaine trade and its attendant negative impacts, the United States has paid considerable attention to external supply disruption. Until at least 2008, the main target of Washington's counternarcotics assistance was Colombia. In line with the deteriorating situation in Mexico, however, the United States has also started to channel a significant amount of security assistance to the Calderón government. In 2008, the George W. Bush administration passed a supplemental budget bill that included $1.6 billion for a so-called Merida Initiative aimed at combating narcotics trafficking and related crime in Central America.

U.S. efforts to fight the Latin American cocaine trade have borne some important results. Thousands of hectares (ha) of coca fields have been destroyed as a result of manual eradication and crop-spraying initiatives. U.S.-trained and -assisted police and military drug units have also scored some notable results, destroying a significant number of hydrochloride and coca-base laboratories in Colombia, and capturing prominent narcotics "kingpins" in Mexico.

That said, Washington's overall counternarcotics assistance program has yet to significantly reduce or undermine the Latin American drug trade. Colombia still constitutes the principal source of cocaine for both the U.S. and global markets, accounting for 90 and 80 percent of respective consumption. There has also been no diminution in drug players operating in Colombia, with FARC remaining a prominent and threatening drug-producing and -trafficking entity and former paramilitaries reemerging as straight crime syndicates.

In Mexico, the situation is even worse, with the northern border states now in the throes of what amounts to a fully fledged narco-war. Moreover, the Merida Initiative, at least as currently formulated, neither addresses the gap between federal and local police forces nor provides assistance at the municipal level to deal with everyday security issues.

Finally, trafficking routes from Colombia and the wider Andean region have, by no means, been curtailed, merely shifting in response to extant interdiction approaches. Indeed, the mosaic of smuggling conduits extending from Latin America is now arguably more complex than ever before, embracing at least five principal transpacific and transatlantic corridors.

Implications for the U.S. Air Force

Although the Latin American drug trade remains primarily a law enforcement issue that is dealt with through various assistance programs managed by the U.S. Department of State, addressing the problem does have direct implications for the U.S. Air Force (USAF). In Colombia and, increasingly, Mexico, Washington is including antinarcotics support as an integral feature of foreign internal defense, and the USAF is already engaged in a number of initiatives with the Joint Interagency Task Force–South (JIATF-S) and U.S. Southern Command (USSOUTHCOM). In addition, there are several relevant roles that the USAF can and should play in boosting the capacity of Mexico— the geographic epicenter for much of what is occurring in the current cocaine trade—to counter drug production and trafficking. Notably, these include providing reliable aerial monitoring assets; training and equipping crews to fly and maintain these platforms; enhancing intelligence, surveillance, and reconnaissance capabilities; and supplying accurate, real-time intelligence (including satellite imagery) to facilitate ground-based and marine interdiction operations. Finally, there are at least four specific measures that the USAF should consider in looking to further hone and adjust its counternarcotics effort in Latin America:

- Augment aerial surveillance over the Pacific–Central American corridor.
- Refine existing standard operating procedures and further institutionalize joint mission statements and protocols regarding drug interdiction.
- Reconsider the policy of aerial fumigation of illegal crops.
- Ensure adequate protection of existing counter–drug-access arrangements in Central America.

Acknowledgments

This study would not have been possible without the collaboration of many people in Latin America and the United States. In particular, the author would like to acknowledge and thank the contributions from Gary Schaffer with JIATF-S in Key West; Perry Holloway and Andrew Erickson with the U.S. Embassy, Bogotá; CAPT James Binniker with the U.S. Coast Guard in Washington, D.C.; CAPT Mark Morris, the U.S. Naval Attaché in Colombia; Roman Ortiz, director of the Fundacio Ideas para la Paz in Bogotá; James Bagley with the University of Miami; and numerous members of the Colombian police, naval, intelligence, and coast guard forces who wish to remain anonymous.

Within RAND, I would like to acknowledge Paula G. Thornhill, director of PAF's Strategy and Doctrine Program, under whose auspices this research was conducted. In addition a special debt of thanks is owed to my assistant, Nancy Good, for help in preparing and editing the manuscript.

Finally, I would like to thank both Beau Kilmer and Samuel Logan for their careful and insightful reviews of the manuscript, which helped to considerably strengthen the final text.

Needless to say, any remaining errors and omissions are the sole responsibility of the author.

Abbreviations

3GEN	third generation
AFSOUTH	Air Forces Southern
AUC	Autodefensas Unidas de Colombia
BACRIM	bandas criminales emergentes
CBP	Customs and Border Patrol
CISEN	Centro de Investigación y Seguridad Nacional, or National Intelligence and Security Center
CNBN	Counter-Narcotics Battalion
CNP	Colombian National Police
DDR	demobilization, disarmament, and reintegration
DEA	Drug Enforcement Administration
DHS	U.S. Department of Homeland Security
DIRAN	Anti-Narcotics Directorate
ELN	Ejército de Liberación Nacional, or National Liberation Army

Erpac	Ejército Revolucionario Popular Anticomunista
EURISPES	Istituto di Studi Politici, Economici e Sociali
FARC	Fuerzas Armadas Revolucionarias de Colombia, or Revolutionary Armed Forces of Colombia
FBI	Federal Bureau of Investigation
FIA	Federal Investigative Agency
FID	foreign internal defense
FY	fiscal year
GAFE	Grupos Aeromóviles de Fuerzas
ha	hectare
HQ USAF/A5X	Deputy Director for Operational Planning, Policy and Strategy, Office of the Deputy Chief of Staff for Operations, Plans and Requirements, Headquarters U.S. Air Force
ICITAP	International Criminal Investigative Training Assistance Program
INL	Bureau of International Narcotics and Law Enforcement Affairs
ISR	intelligence, surveillance, and reconnaissance
JIATF-S	Joint Interagency Task Force–South
MAOC	Maritime Analysis and Operations Centre
MS-13	Mara Salvatrucha–13
MT	metric ton
NDV	Norte del Valle

NGO	nongovernmental organization
nm	nautical mile
ONDCP	Office of National Drug Control Policy
PAF	Project AIR FORCE
SL	Sendero Luminoso (Shining Path)
SPSS	self-propelled semisubmersible
UNHCR	United Nations High Commissioner for Refugees
UNODC	United Nations Office on Drugs and Crime
USAF	U.S. Air Force
USCG	U.S. Coast Guard
USSOUTHCOM	U.S. Southern Command
YTD	year to date

CHAPTER ONE

Introduction

Transnational crime remains a particularly serious problem in Latin America, affecting numerous states both in and beyond the region and having severe repercussions for political, economic, and human security. Although a range of issues confront policymakers and decisionmakers, most are, in some way or another, connected with the drug trade. This particular threat has emerged as a prominent feature on the U.S. national security agenda, reflecting the emergence of new groups involved in production and trafficking, the development of more-sophisticated smuggling methods, and the sharp rise of intercartel violence to the immediate south of the U.S. border. In Colombia and, increasingly, Mexico, Washington is including antinarcotics assistance as an integral feature of foreign internal defense (FID) and, in both countries, continues to underwrite extremely expansive interdiction efforts.

This monograph examines the scope and dimensions of the Latin American drug trade. It first discusses key developments in cocaine production and trafficking, focusing on trends in cultivation and processing and the principal "players" involved in the manufacture and movement of drugs out of the Andean region. The monograph then examines the main methods and routes that are used to ship narcotics between source, transit, and consumption countries and the principal consequences that are associated with this manifestation of transnational crime. Finally, the study considers specific implications for the U.S. Air Force (USAF) and offers some initial recommendations on how its counternarcotics strategy in Latin America can be adjusted and further refined.

CHAPTER TWO

Production and Trafficking Routes

Cocaine

Colombia currently accounts for the vast bulk of cocaine produced in Latin America and remains the principal supplier for both the United States (accounting for 90 percent of consumption) and the worldwide market (accounting for 80 percent of consumption).[1] In 2009, 116,000 hectares (ha) of coca leaf were cultivated in the country, yielding an estimated 270 metric tons (MT) of pure cocaine (see Table 2.1).[2]

Two other important cocaine sources exist in Latin America: Peru (cultivation concentrated in Alto Huallaga, Apurimac-Ene, and La

---

[1] Author interview, Bogotá, March 2009.

[2] Data for drug production in Latin America are derived from U.S. Department of State statistics. The other main source of information on the illegal drug market is the United Nations Office on Drugs and Crime (UNODC). Discrepancies in the two data sources are not uncommon, which reflects the inherent fragility of supply-side estimates. However, figures can be used to indicate general trends and are necessary to provide some empirical basis for the analysis. To ensure a measure of consistency, statistics from the U.S. Department of State are used in this monograph, although reference to other sources is made when relevant. For discussions and critiques of supply-side estimates as a source of empirical analysis, see Peter H. Reuter and Victoria A. Greenfield, "Measuring Global Drug Markets: How Good Are the Numbers and Why Should We Care About Them?" *World Economics*, Vol. 2, No. 4, October–December 2001, pp. 159–173; Daniel Mejia and Carlos Esteban Posada, *Cocaine Production and Trafficking: What Do We Know?* Washington, D.C.: World Bank Policy Research Working Paper 4618, May 1, 2008; Beau Kilmer and Stijn Hoorens, *Understanding Illicit Drug Markets, Supply-Reduction Efforts, and Drug-Related Crime in the European Union*, Santa Monica, Calif.: RAND Corporation, TR-755-EC, 2010; and Beau Kilmer and Rosalie Liccardo Pacula, *Estimating the Size of the Global Drug Market: A Demand-Side Approach: Report 2*, Santa Monica, Calif.: RAND Corporation, TR-711-EC, 2009.

Table 2.1
Colombian Coca Cultivation (in hectares) and Potential Cocaine Production (in MT), 2005–2009

	2005	2006	2007	2008	2009
Coca cultivation	144,000	157,200	167,000	119,000	116,000
Potential cocaine production	500	515	485	295	270

SOURCE: U.S. Department of State, 2011.

Convención y Lares) and Bolivia (cultivation concentrated in Chapare, the Yungas of La Paz, and Apolo). In 2009, these countries generated enough base material to respectively produce 225 MT and 195 MT of refined product (see Tables 2.2 and 2.3), figures that the U.S. State Department expected to stay largely constant for 2009.[3] It should be noted, however, that UNODC recorded a 7-percent increase in Peruvian output during 2009, with the increase largely attributed to weak internal interdiction efforts, as well as the "displacement effect" of crop eradication in Colombia.[4] According to Jaime Antezana, a senior secu-

Table 2.2
Peruvian Coca Cultivation (in hectares) and Potential Cocaine Production (in MT), 2005–2007

	2005	2006	2007	2008	2009
Coca cultivation	34,000	42,000	36,000	41,000	40,000
Potential cocaine production	240	245	210	215[a]	225

SOURCE: U.S. Department of State, 2011.

[a] According to the U.S. State Department, the decline in Peruvian production between 2005 and 2008 despite the increase in cultivation is attributed to interdiction and eradication programs, which are estimated to have reduced potential cocaine production by 30 percent.

---

[3] Author interviews, Cartagena, November 2008. See also Christopher Aaron, "Coca Production Is on the Increase in Bolivia, Peru," *Jane's Intelligence Review*, January, August 2005, p. 40; and Simon Romero, "Cocaine Trade Helps Rebels Reignite War in Peru," *New York Times*, March 17, 2009a.

[4] See United Nations Office on Drugs and Crime, *World Drug Report 2010*, 2010.

Table 2.3
Bolivian Coca Cultivation (in hectares) and Potential Cocaine Production (in MT), 2005–2007

	2005	2006	2007	2008	2009
Coca cultivation	26,500	25,800	29,500	32,000	35,000
Potential cocaine production	115	115	130	195	195[a]

SOURCE: U.S. Department of State, 2011.

[a] According to the U.S. State Department, the surge in potential cocaine production relative to the only-modest rise in cultivation is attributed to the adoption of more-efficient processing methods and the increased presence of Colombian and Mexican drug groups in the country.

rity analyst with the Catholic University in Lima, if current trends continue, the country could surpass Colombia as the world's largest producer of coca leaf by 2010.[5]

There is also some concern about higher cultivation levels occurring in Bolivia due to the policies of the current La Paz government. Not only has Evo Morales sanctioned the licit production of 40,000 acres of coca to meet indigenous demand (paralleling policies in Peru, where growing the plant is largely legal), in a similar vein to an earlier Venezuelan example (see below); he suspended all cooperation with the Drug Enforcement Administration (DEA) in 2008 for allegedly funding "criminal groups."[6]

Between 60 and 65 percent of all Latin American cocaine is trafficked to the United States, the bulk of which is smuggled via the eastern Pacific/Central American corridor. The remainder is sent through the Caribbean island chain, with the Dominican Republic, Puerto

---

[5] Simon Romero, "Coca Production Makes a Comeback in Peru," *New York Times*, June 13, 2010a.

[6] Author interviews, Bogotá, March 2009. See also "Bolivia Expels U.S. Diplomat," Associated Press, March 9, 2009. In addition to suspending cooperation with DEA, the Morales government expelled U.S. Ambassador Philip Goldberg and, in 2009, ordered Second Secretary Francisco Martínez out of the country for allegedly conspiring with opposition groups.

Rico, and Haiti acting as the main transshipment hubs.[7] In both cases, Mexico serves as the principal point of entry to mainland United States, with the country presently accounting for as much as 90 percent of all illicit imports to the United States (see Figure 2.1).[8]

Increasing amounts of Latin American cocaine are now also being sent to Europe (see Figure 2.2). Most consignments are smuggled in container vessels and dispatched directly to ports in Spain (Barce-

Figure 2.1
Mexican Drug-Trafficking Routes

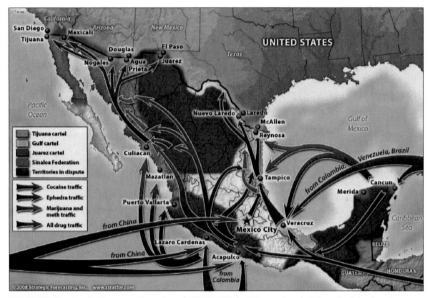

SOURCE: Strategic Forecasting, Inc. (STRATFOR), "Organized Crime in Mexico," March 11, 2008. Used with permission.
RAND *MG1076-2.1*

---

[7] Author interviews, Washington, D.C., January and February 2009, and Bogotá, March 2009.

[8] Author interviews, Miami, Cartagena, Bogotá, and Key West, November 2008–March 2009. See also United Nations Office on Drugs and Crime, *World Drug Report 2008*, 2008, and Bureau for International Narcotics and Law Enforcement Affairs, "Counternarcotics and Law Enforcement Country Program: Mexico," fact sheet, Washington, D.C.: U.S. Department of State, January 20, 2009.

Figure 2.2
Colombian Cocaine-Trafficking Routes
Direct to Europe

RAND *MG1076-2.2*

lona), Portugal (Lisbon), the Netherlands (Rotterdam), and Belgium (Antwerp).[9] The growing emphasis on Europe reflects higher street prices than those in the United States[10] (see Table 2.4) and shifting consumer demand patterns toward this particular narcotic (and derivates, such as crack).[11] Based on prevalence rates in 2008, the United States accounted for roughly 44 percent of global cocaine consumption, Europe 25 percent. In the latter case, the UK constitutes the

---

[9]   Author interview, Key West, March 2009. In 2006, for instance, 9.4 tons of cocaine that had been shipped to Lisbon was smuggled in containers of frozen squid. Seven months later, Spanish authorities apprehended a Venezuelan-flagged vessel that had 2.5 tons of cocaine onboard, which subsequently led to the dismantling of one of the biggest drug gangs in the country's northwestern region of Galicia. See Andy Webb-Vidal, "Cocaine Coasts: Venezuela and West Africa's Drug Axis," *Jane's Intelligence Review*, February 2009a, p. 49.

[10]   According to UNODC, this price differential is largely a result of the relative strength of the euro to the U.S. dollar (adjusted for inflation) as opposed to changes in the market itself. See UNODC, 2010, p. 171.

[11]   Author interviews, Bogotá, March 2009.

Table 2.4
Comparative Estimated Values of Latin American Cocaine Exports to Consumers in North America and Europe

Region	Estimated Value (millions of U.S. dollars)
North America: low estimate	15
North America: high estimate	23
Europe: low estimate	30
Europe: high estimate	45[a]

SOURCE: Kilmer and Pacula, 2009, p. 70.

[a] Obviously, the import price of cocaine in Europe is contingent on location and trafficking method. Unfortunately, there is no average estimate for the continent as a whole. These figures are based on interviews with drug dealers and statistics provided by law enforcement. See Mark Schoofs and Paulo Prada, "Cocaine Boom in Europe Fuels New Laundering Tactics," *Wall Street Journal*, January 16, 2008, and Matrix Knowledge Group, *The Illicit Drug Trade in the United Kingdom*, London: Home Office, 2007.

largest cocaine market on the continent in absolute terms, with usage among the general population standing at 1.2 million in 2009.[12]

The more-common route, however, runs via hubs in West Africa, especially Sierra Leone, Guinea-Bissau, Guinea, Ghana, Mali, and Senegal (see Figure 2.3). All of these countries have weak judicial institutions, lack the resources for effective (or, indeed, even rudimentary) coastal surveillance, and are beset by endemic corruption—making them ideal transshipment hubs for moving narcotics out of Latin America.[13] According to U.S. officials, between 25 and 35 percent of all Andean cocaine consumed in Europe arrives from one of these

---

[12] See UNODC, 2010, p. 177. See also Judd, Terri, "Drug Mule Pensioners: The New Couriers of Choice," *Independent* (UK), December 4, 2008. The highest prevalence rate is in Scotland, with around 3.7 percent of the population estimated to be taking cocaine. Actual figures might be higher because general demographic surveys tend to miss large numbers of heavy users.

[13] Guinea-Bissau, one of the poorest countries in Africa, is thought to be the primary transit point in West Africa because of its geography, lack of resources for coastal surveillance, and exceptionally weak, corrupt institutions.

**Figure 2.3
Colombian Cocaine Routes to Europe via
West Africa**

RAND *MG1076-2.3*

states.[14] A 2008 report by UNODC similarly estimated that at least 50 tons of Colombian drugs pass through West Africa every year, with cocaine seizures doubling annually from 1.32 tons in 2005 to 3.16 tons in 2006 to 6.46 tons in 2007.[15] In the words of Antonio María Costa, the former executive director of UNODC, the illicit trade has become so endemic that it has now effectively turned "the Gold Coast into the Coke Coast."[16]

The majority of the Colombian cocaine that is trafficked to Europe, either directly or via West Africa, is exported from Venezuela. Consignments are almost exclusively sent by sea and follow what has become colloquially known as Highway 10—a reference to the 10th degree of latitude that connects the northern part of Latin America

---

[14] Author interviews, Washington, D.C., January and February 2009, and Key West, March 2009.

[15] UNODC, 2008, p. 79; Webb-Vidal, 2009a, p. 49.

[16] Cited in Webb-Vidal, 2009a, p. 47.

with its closest point on the African continent across the Atlantic.[17] In an attempt to disrupt these flows, several European governments created a dedicated intergovernmental counternarcotics organization in 2006. Known as the Maritime Analysis and Operations Centre (MAOC) and headquartered in Lisbon, this body has the remit to disrupt cocaine consignments being sent from Latin America in an arc that stretches 12,000 kilometers from Iceland to the Cape of Good Hope in South Africa. MAOC blends law enforcement and military, fusing and disseminating intelligence to avail coordinated drug interdiction by seven participating states: France, Ireland, Italy, the Netherlands, Portugal, Spain, and the UK (Europol, Germany, and Canada all hold observer status).[18]

Only small amounts of cocaine are trafficked from Venezuela by air—so-called narco avionetas—with two main corridors in evidence: one to Central America (accounting for 68 illegal air tracks in 2008) and one to Espínola (accounting for 114 illegal air tracks in 2008). In most cases, single-engine Cessnas are used, which are capable of transporting loads of up to 400–500 kg (0.5 MT) at a time. According to U.S. officials, around 20 percent of the cocaine that is flown to Central America is subsequently repackaged and sent to West Africa or Europe.[19]

Venezuela's role as a primary transshipment hub has expanded considerably since 2005, when President Hugo Chávez terminated all cooperation with DEA on the grounds that its agents had been engaged in espionage activities against his government. In addition, there is widespread speculation that officials in the Caracas military and intelligence establishment have been prepared to materially assist the Revolutionary Armed Forces of Colombia (FARC) as a proxy against Colombia by routinely allowing the group to traffic cocaine across the state's territory. In September 2008, Washington named two serving and one former Venezuelan official as complicit in FARC's

---

[17] Joseph Kirschke, "The Coke Coast: Cocaine's New Venezuelan Address," *World Politics Review*, September 11, 2008.

[18] Andy Webb-Vidal, "Secret Weapon," Jane's Intelligence Review, April 2009b, p. 58.

[19] Author interviews, Key West, March 2009.

cocaine activities: Hugo Armando Carvajal Barrios (chief of the Military Intelligence Directorate), Henry de Jesús Rangel Silva (director of Intelligence and Prevention Services), and Ramón Rodríguez (a former justice and interior minister).[20]

The overall magnitude of narcotics passing through Venezuela is not known but is believed to be extensive. Figures produced by the U.S. State Department, for instance, show that at least 58.1 tons of the cocaine seized in West Africa during 2007 originated from the republic, which, by its own estimates, was more than 16 times the volume from Colombia. Drug seizures in Venezuela have also dropped since the abrogation of the DEA cooperation agreement in 2005 (see Table 2.5), which U.S. authorities insist merely confirms that the state is complicit in narco-trafficking and is now the premier transit zone in Latin America for cocaine bound for Europe.[21]

In addition to Venezuela, Brazil, Argentina, and Uruguay constitute significant export hubs for shipments across the Atlantic (see Figures 2.4 and 2.5). This is especially true of Peruvian and Bolivian cocaine, which, according to U.S. officials, is predominantly routed through one of these three states (90 percent in the case of Bolivia and 70 percent in the case of Peru).[22] Colombians and, increasingly, Mexicans working in conjunction with Italian and local crime syndicates based in the Brazilian favelas of Rio de Janeiro, Sao Paulo, Salvador, and Recife, as well as Buenos Aires and Montevideo, appear to be at the forefront of these consignments, reputedly seeking to tap a Euro-

Table 2.5
Cocaine Seizures in Venezuela, 2000–2007

	2000	2001	2002	2003	2004	2005	2006	2007
Amount (tons)	14.31	13.39	17.79	32.25	31.22	58.44	38.94	31.79

SOURCE: Venezuelan National Anti-Drugs Office.

---

[20] Author interviews, Cartagena, November 2008, and Bogotá, March 2009.

[21] Author interviews, Bogotá, March 2009. See also Webb-Vidal, 2009a, pp. 48–49.

[22] Author interviews, Bogotá, March 2009.

Figure 2.4
Peruvian and Bolivian Cocaine Routes to
Europe

RAND *MG1076-2.4*

Figure 2.5
Peruvian and Bolivian Cocaine Routes to
Europe via West Africa

RAND *MG1076-2.5*

pean market that favors Bolivian cocaine.[23] As with Venezuela, shipments are dispatched either directly to ports in Portugal, Spain, the Netherlands, and Belgium, or via littoral states off the West African coast, where Guinea-Bissau allegedly acts as the key point of entry.[24]

Opiates

Besides cocaine, Colombia also represents a relatively important source of North America opiates. According to State Department officials in Bogotá, the country traditionally accounted for around half of the white heroin consumed east of the Mississippi.[25] Since 2003, however, overall poppy cultivation in the country has dropped significantly as a result of a concerted aerial and manual eradication effort. In 2008, Colombia produced around 1,000 hectares of poppies, providing sufficient base for around 15 MT of oven-dried opium and 1.9 MT of refined heroin (see Table 2.6).[26]

As noted, the bulk of Colombian opiates are sent to the United States. In common with cocaine, the main trafficking route extends up the eastern Pacific to Mexico. Although the latter country has traditionally acted as a shipper, in recent years, it has begun to emerge as a prominent opiate source in its own right, generating 105 MT of black tar and 38 MT of pure heroin in 2008 (see Table 2.7) and now thought

---

[23] The extent of these drug shipments is considerable. Between June and July 2008, for instance, nearly $1 million worth of cocaine and coca paste was seized by the Argentine Customs and Coast Guard, most of which was being smuggled to Uruguay, via the San Francisco stream, for subsequent export to Europe. By the end of July, authorities had seized 34 kg of pure cocaine and 2 kg of coca paste. See "Riverine Operations Set Sights on Drug Traffickers," *Dialogo*, Vol. 18, No. 4, 2008, pp. 26–27.

[24] Author interviews, Bogotá and Key West, March 2009. See also "Riverine Operations Set Sights on Drug Traffickers," 2008, p. 27, and Robert Munks, "Brazilian Police Officers Storm the Favelas," *Jane's Intelligence Review*, February 2009b, p. 6.

[25] Author interview, Bogotá, March 2009.

[26] The high point of opium cultivation in Colombia was 2001, when a little over 7,000 ha of poppy fields were harvested; the 2007 figure, therefore, represents a decrease of about 65 percent (author interviews, Bogotá, March 2009).

Table 2.6
Colombian Poppy Cultivation (in hectares) and Potential Heroin Production
(in MT), 2005–2009

	2005	2006	2007	2008	2009
Poppy cultivation	N/A	2,300	1,000	1,000	TBD
Potential oven-dried opium production	N/A	37	15	15	TBD
Potential pure heroin production	N/A	4.6	1.9	1.9	TBD

SOURCE: U.S. Department of State, *International Narcotics Control Strategy Report*, March 2010.

Table 2.7
Mexican Poppy Cultivation (in hectares) and Potential Heroin Production
(in MT), 2005–2009

	2005	2006	2007	2008	2009
Poppy cultivation	3,300	5,100	N/A	6,900	15,000[a]
Potential black tar production	22	36	50	105	TBD
Potential pure heroin production	8	13	18	38	TBD

SOURCE: U.S. Department of State, 2010.
[a] This was the year-to-date (YTD) figure up to November 5, 2009.

to be the main supplier for the U.S. western market.[27] According to U.S. officials, this development reflects both a demand for higher-quality and purer opiates, as well as the failure of poppy-eradication efforts in Mexico.[28]

---

[27] Author interviews, Miami, November 2008, and Bogotá, March 2009. See also John P. Sullivan and Adam Elkus, "State of Siege: Mexico's Criminal Insurgency," *Small Wars Journal*, August 2008, p. 3; Central Intelligence Agency, 2008.

[28] Author interviews, Cartagena, November 2008. Apart from opiates, Mexico has also long acted as an important source of marijuana (midgrade and hydroponic) and methamphetamines sold in the United States. For more on this illegal trade, see Oscar Becerra, "Black Ice: Methamphetamines on the Rise in Mexico," *Jane's Intelligence Review*, September 2009b, and Solomon Moore, "Tougher Border Can't Stop Mexican Marijuana Cartels," *New York Times*, February 1, 2009.

CHAPTER THREE

Main Players

Colombia

FARC currently represents the principal narco-player in Colombia. The group was established in 1966 under the leadership of Manuel Marulanda (alias "Sureshot") with the purported aim of seizing national power through a protracted people's war—although the bulk of its agenda has tended to focus on more pragmatic goals, such as land redistribution, reform of the security forces, and empowerment of the peasant classes. The organization is estimated to have around 9,000 combatants (2009 figure) and control of seven regional blocs (see Table 3.1) that oversee an estimated 71 fronts across the country.[1] In addition, it has an available reinforcement surge capacity consisting of 15 independent companies and several mobile columns.

FARC is involved in all aspects of the drug trade, from production through refining to trafficking, and is thought to earn anywhere between US$200 million and US$300 million per year from these activities (which is thought to equate to roughly half of its overall operational budget).[2] Historically, most of this income was used

---

[1] This stands in stark contrast to the 16,000–18,000 combatants that made up FARC in 2001.

[2] Bilal Y. Saab and Alexandra W. Taylor, "Criminality and Armed Groups: A Comparative Study of FARC and Paramilitary Groups in Colombia," *Studies in Conflict and Terrorism*, Vol. 32, No. 6, June 2009, pp. 455–475, p. 463; Alexandra Guaqueta, "The Colombian Conflict: Political and Economic Dimensions," in Karen Ballentine and Jake Sherman, eds., *The Political Economy of Armed Conflict: Beyond Greed and Grievance*, Boulder, Colo.: Lynne Rienner Publishers, 2003, pp. 73–106, p. 93; "Colombian FARC Insurgency Could Face

Table 3.1
Revolutionary Armed Forces of Colombia Blocs and Geographical Areas of Influence

Bloc	Commander	Area of Influence
Eastern	Granobles (a.k.a. Noe Suarez Rojas)	Arauca, Guaviare, Meta, Vichada
Western	Pablo Catatumbo	Cauca, Valle del Cauca, Narino
Southern	Joaquin Gomez, Fabian Ramirez (a.k.a. Jose Benito Cabrera Cuevas)	Cqueta, Huila, Putumayo
Central	Alfonso Cano, Jeronimo (a.k.a. Raul Duarte)	Huila, Quindio, Risaralda, Tolima
Middle Magdalena	Pastor Alape (a.k.a. Felix Antonio Munoz Lascarro)	Antioquia, Bolivar, Boyaca, Cesar, Norde del Santander, Santander
Caribbean	Bertulfo (Emilio Carbrera Diaz)	Cesar, Magdalena, Sucre
Northwestern (also known as Ivan Rios bloc)	Ivan Marquez	Antioquia, Choco, Cordoba

SOURCE: Andy Webb-Vidal, "Fight the Future," *Jane's Intelligence Review*, September 2008, p. 18.

to underwrite and sustain FARC's insurgent war against Bogotá. In recent years, however, it appears that elements in the organization have increasingly turned to narcotics as an exclusive economic endeavor, with greed and profit rather than politics and ideology being the main motivational drivers.

Several fronts are thought to be involved exclusively in the narcotics trade. Notable in this regard is the 16th, which DEA has directly implicated in deals involving international cocaine traffickers operat-

---

Its Most Serious Crisis," Voice of America, July 8, 2008. It should be noted that this figure is the high-end estimate. UNODC, for instance, estimates that total profits accruing from Colombian cocaine exports are probably no more than $2.4 billion, which would mean that FARC's share would be considerably less than $2 billion to $3 billion. See UNODC, 2010, p. 79.

ing out of Brazil, Peru, and Mexico.[3] Overall, by 2005, it was thought that some 65 of FARC's 110 fronts were involved in some aspect of the drug trade.[4] Indeed, several commentators now believe that FARC as a whole is showing signs of degenerating into a purely crime-based entity, arguing that this reflects its faltering militant campaign and fits with growing evidence that the group has entrenched itself with Mexican syndicates (see below) to traffic drugs to the U.S. market.[5]

Certainly, FARC is weaker as an insurgent force today than it has ever been. The group's current total membership is around half that in 2001. According to Colombian Ministry of National Defense figures, between 2006 and 2008, the group lost 17,274 combatants—5,316 through voluntary demobilizations and the remainder through captures and casualties.[6] That said, it is too early to conclude that FARC has fully abandoned its insurgent agenda. More likely, it reflects growing command-and-control problems that have confronted the organization as a result of the loss of some of its key leaders in 2008, including Marulanda,[7] Luis Edgar Devia-Silva (a.k.a. Raul Reyes, the group's chief ideologue), Manuel Munoz-Ortiz (a.k.a. Ivan Rios, head of the Central Block), Alfonso Cano (who took over from Marulanda fol-

---

[3] The 16th Front's long-time leader, Tomas Molina (a.k.a. Negro Acacio), was killed during a Colombian bombing raid against his camp in September 2007. He was known to have been a close associate of Brazilian drug dealer Fernando Beira-Mar and gained notoriety for participating in an illegal FARC arms deal involving 10,000 AK-47s that had been arranged through Vladimiro Montesinos—an intelligence adviser to former Peruvian president Alberto Fujimori. For more on the latter incident, see Joe Wessely, "Peru: Former Spy Chief Vladimiro Montesinos Gets 20-Year Sentence for Arms Sale to Colombian Rebels," *Latin America Data Base*, Latin American and Iberian Institute, University of New Mexico, October 6, 2006.

[4] Author interviews, Bogotá, March 2009. See also Saab and Taylor, 2009, p. 465; Steinitz, Mark S., "The Terrorism and Drug Connection in Latin America's Andean Region," *Policy Papers on the Americas*, Vol. XIII, Study 5, July 2002, pp. 32–33; and International Crisis Group, 2005.

[5] Author interviews, Miami and Cartagena, November 2008.

[6] See Saab and Taylor, 2009, pp. 459–460, and Ministry of National Defense, "The FARC at their Worst Moment in History," September 15, 2008, pp. 9–10.

[7] Marulanda died of a heart attack in May 2008; it is widely assumed that this was triggered by the stress associated with FARC setbacks at the hands of the Colombian Army.

lowing his death), Gerardo Aguilar (a.k.a. Cesar, a senior cadre in the organization's secretariat), Alexander Farfan (a.k.a. Enrique Gafas, also a prominent member of the secretariat), and Jorge Briceño (a.k.a. Mono Joyjoy, FARC's second in command).[8]

Paramilitaries also play a role in the Colombian drug trade. These organizations originally emerged as civil defense units to safeguard the population in areas where the state was unable to provide sufficient security on its own. In 1996, most of the then-independent paramilitary groups agreed to coalesce under the umbrella of the Autodefensas Unidas de Colombia (AUC), which presented itself to landowners and businesspeople plundered by guerrillas as an "anticommunist advance guard in defense of private property and free enterprise."[9] By the end of the 1990s, however, the AUC had effectively morphed into a dedicated narcotics-trafficking entity, emerging as the principal smuggler of Colombian cocaine to the U.S. market.[10]

Most paramilitaries surrendered their weapons in a government-brokered demobilization, disarmament, and reintegration (DDR) deal that was completed in 2006. The terms of the agreement, which originated from the 2003 Santa Fé de Ralito Accord and was later enshrined in the Peace and Justice Law (Law 975) of July 2005, limited jail terms for the highest-ranking members of the AUC to eight years if they confessed the entirety of their crimes and returned all stolen property. More-junior paramilitaries that demobilized were enrolled in an 18- to 24-month program that provided them with a stipend, living accommodations, counseling, and help with reincorporating into main-

---

[8] Simon Romero, "Settling of Crisis Makes Winners of Andes Nations, While Rebels Lose Ground," *New York Times*, March 9, 2008; Jerry McDermott, "Colombia Reports Death of FARC Leader," *Daily Telegraph* (UK), May 27, 2008; Simon Romero, "Rebels' Second in Command Has Been Killed, Colombia Says," *New York Times*, September 23, 2010b.

[9] Mauricio Romero, "Changing Identities and Contested Settings: Regional Elites and the Paramilitaries in Colombia," *International Journal of Politics, Culture and Society*, Vol. 14, No. 1, 2000, pp. 51–69, p. 66; Saab and Taylor, 2009, p. 461.

[10] For an overview of AUC activity in the drug trade during this period, see Angel Rabasa and Peter Chalk, *Colombian Labyrinth: The Synergy of Drugs and Insurgency and Its Implications for Regional Stability*, Santa Monica, Calif.: RAND Corporation, MR-1339-AF, 2001, Chapter Five.

stream society. More than 30,000 adhered to these stipulations and surrendered their weapons as part of the DDR process. Problematically, however, the government estimated that the AUC had no more than 12,000 members, and, as a result, the DDR program was quickly overwhelmed—something that was compounded by the marginal support it received from the private sector. More than 75 percent of those who entered the program never received a job and complained that Bogotá had not lived up to its side of the bargain. Initial dissatisfaction translated into widespread disillusionment, driving many to join preexisting criminal gangs (which were never covered by the DDR deal and which, as a result, remained intact).[11]

These reconfigured entities, which are euphemistically referred to as bandas criminales emergentes (criminal groups, or simply BACRIM) now focus exclusively on the drug trade and make no pretense of seeking political or ideological objectives.[12] Commenting on this feature of the reemergent paramilitary threat, the influential nongovernmental organization Fundación Seguridad y Democracia (Security and Democracy Foundation) issued a statement in June 2008 specifically stating that "the common characteristic of all [the BACRIM] is involvement in drug trafficking and a host of other illicit activities."[13]

According to the Intelligence Directorate of the Colombian National Police, more than 5,300 reconstituted paramilitaries have been arrested since 2006, with a further 1,100 killed in combat with the authorities. Based on these official figures, the total number of BACRIM members over the past three years has probably fluctuated

---

[11] Sebastian Chaskel and Michael Bustamante, "Colombia's Precarious Progress," *Current History*, February 2008, pp. 80–81; Andy Webb-Vidal, "Back from the Dead," *Jane's Intelligence Review*, May 2009c, pp. 39, 43; Saab and Taylor, 2009, pp. 462–463; Liz Harper, "Colombian Congress Approves Controversial Bill to Revive Peace Talks," *Online News Hour*, June 24, 2005; Douglas Porch and María José Rasmussen, "Demobilization of Paramilitaries in Colombia: Transformation or Transition?" *Studies in Conflict and Terrorism*, Vol. 31, No. 6, June 2008, pp. 520–540, p. 528; Ralph Rozema, "Urban DDR-Processes: Paramilitaries and Criminal Networks in Medellín, Colombia," *Journal of Latin American Studies*, Vol. 40, No. 3, 2008, pp. 423–452, pp. 444, 448.

[12] Author interviews, Washington, D.C., January 2009.

[13] Cited in Webb-Vidal, 2009c, p. 41.

around the 5,000 mark.[14] Government authorities have identified 11 main gangs that account for the bulk of these individuals (down from 33–67 between 2006 and 2007), four of which remained at the forefront of national security concern:

- the Don Mario gang, which has an estimated 1,077 men under arms. It is the largest and most-influential of the reemerging paramilitary gangs, although the organization suffered from the April 2009 arrest of its leader, Daniel Rendón Herrera (described by the police as the country's "most wanted criminal").
- the Ejército Revolucionario Popular Anticomunista (Erpac), which has around 725 members. It is led by Pedro Olivero (a.k.a. Cuchillo or the knife), although the real financial power behind the organization is alleged to be a local narco-trafficker named Loco Barrera.
- the Rastrojos, which have around 1,200 members who are subdivided into seven geographical units: Nariño, Cauca, Putumayo, Cesar, Choco, Norte de Santander, and Santander. Although Colombian police do not think that the gang falls under the authority of a single leader, they believe that Luis Calle Serna runs the group's money-laundering and white-collar crime activities (through a subgroup known as Los Comba) while Diego Pérez Henao heads up its armed wing.
- Los Paisas is the smallest of the four gangs, with approximately 172 operatives based out of Sucre and Córdoba. In common with the Rastrojos, Los Paisas has no identified commander but is thought to act as the armed muscle of the Envigado Office—a multipronged crime syndicate located just outside Medellín.[15]

---

[14] It should be noted that nongovernmental organizations (NGOs) have cast doubt on the veracity of government data, arguing Bogotá has a vested interest in downplaying the extent of the paramilitary problem to safeguard the perceived success of its demobilization program. Figures released by these organizations put the true number anywhere between 6,000 and 10,000 (author interview, Bogotá, March 2009; see also Webb-Vidal, 2009c, pp. 43, 48).

[15] Author interviews, Bogotá, March 2009. See also Jerry McDermott, "Generational Shift: Colombia's Evolving Drug Cartel," *Jane's Intelligence Review*, February 2010, pp. 43–44;

The former Uribe administration sanctioned the national police with a specific mandate to hunt down each of the groups. As part of this endeavor, a joint verification mechanism was established in 2006 to coordinate law enforcement efforts with other government agencies and departments. At the time of this writing, this umbrella organization incorporated the ministries of Defense, Justice, and Interior; the attorney general's office; and three police national directorates (intelligence, criminal investigations, and the gendarmerie).[16]

A third player on the Colombian drug scene is the Norte del Valle (NDV). The syndicate originally arose to prominence in the ashes of the demise of the Medellín and Cali cartels in the 1990s and, for a time, was the country's most-powerful narcotics crime group. According to U.S. officials, the NDV smuggled more than 1.2 million pounds (or 500 MT) of cocaine, worth some $10 billion, to the United States between 1990 and 2004. The cartel has progressively diminished in prominence, however, due to growing factionalism in its ranks and the capture or elimination of some of its leading personalities. These included the NDV supreme "godfather" and one of the most-wanted men in Colombia, Diego Montoya (a.k.a. Don Diego). Although clearly weakened by infighting and arrests, NDV cells continue to play a role in drug trafficking, acting primarily as specialized subcontractors to whoever is willing to pay for their services.[17]

Webb-Vidal, 2009c, p. 40; Chris Kraul, "Colombia Police Arrest Major Drug Figure," *Los Angeles Times*, April 16, 2009b.

[16] Author interviews, Bogotá, March 2009. See also Chris Kraul, "Paramilitary Groups Still Spread Terror Among Colombia's People," *Los Angeles Times*, December 5, 2008c; Chris Kraul, "New Gangs Run Colombians Off Their Land," *Los Angeles Times*, December 3, 2008b; and Juan Forero, "Deep in the Colombian Jungle, Coca Still Thrives," National Public Radio, April 3, 2007.

[17] Author interviews, Bogotá, March 2009. See also "America's Most Wanted Drug Smuggler Diego Montoya Caught in Colombia," Associated Press, September 10, 2007; "Norte del Valle Cartel Is Finished: Naranjo," *Colombia Reports*, December 12, 2008; Chris Kraul, "Colombian Drug Lord Killed," *Los Angeles Times*, February 2, 2008a. Other top leaders neutralized have been Juan Carlos Ramírez Abadía (a.k.a. El Chupeta, captured in Brazil in August 2007), Carlos José Robayo Escobar (a.k.a. Macaw, caught in 2005), and Wilber Alirio Fajardo Varela (shot dead in Venezuela in 2008).

Finally, there are indications that the National Liberation Army (ELN) is now becoming more-intimately involved in cocaine production and trafficking. Students from the University of Santander founded the group in 1964, seeking to emulate a Cuban-style revolution in Colombia. At its height, the organization could count on about 5,000 members who operated from five frentes de guerra (war fronts) mostly concentrated in an extended region that stretched from the middle Magdalena Valley to the Venezuelan border. The insurgent threat emanating from ELN has steadily declined over the past nine years, however, reflecting defections, losses at the hands of the Colombian security forces (which combined have seen their numbers shrink by as much as one-third), and a steady reduction of territory as a result of protracted conflicts with both FARC and the AUC.[18]

Traditionally, most of the ELN's criminal income was derived from kidnap for ransom and extorting protection money from energy firms (oil, gas, and coal) and mining companies (gold and emeralds). By the turn of the millennium, the group was thought to have earned approximately $150 million from these criminal pursuits, 30 percent from kidnapping and 70 percent from extortion.[19] According to U.S. and Colombian officials, however, the group increasingly moved away from these activities during the early 2000s and has now reoriented most of its fundraising toward the far more-lucrative drug trade—with most activity concentrated along the northern Pacific coast. Although senior members continue to profess their commitment to Castroite Marxist ideology, the main driver for involvement in these activities appears to be straight profit. Irrespective of motive, however, the ELN has yet to make any real definitive inroad into the Colombian cocaine industry, its influence being constrained by ongoing police and mili-

---

[18] Rabasa and Chalk, 2001, pp. 30–31.

[19] See Alex McDougall, "State Power and Its Implications for Civil War in Colombia," *Studies in Conflict and Terrorism*, Vol. 32, No. 4, April 2009, pp. 322–345, p. 338; and Richani, Nazih, *Systems of Violence: The Political Economy of War and Peace in Colombia*, Albany, N.Y.: State University of New York Press, 2002, p. 170.

tary harassment, as well as sustained competition from stronger and better-connected FARC and paramilitary rivals.[20]

Besides FARC, paramilitaries, the NDV, and ELN, there are an estimated 350 smaller drug syndicates in Colombia, reflecting a highly dispersed and atomized "industry." Most of these groups, known as "baby cartels,"[21] have compartmentalized their responsibilities, with some overseeing smuggling routes to Mexico, some controlling jungle-based processing laboratories, and some dealing with cultivation and in-country transportation of coca base.[22] At the time of this writing, there had been no moves on the part of these smaller cartels to expand and consolidate greater market control over their respective operations. Law enforcement officials concede that the resulting patchwork arrangement is proving exceedingly difficult to disrupt and will probably remain in place irrespective of any success that is made to counter the narcotics-related activities of FARC.[23]

Peru and Bolivia

The Peruvian and Bolivian drug trade is largely dispersed among a plethora of amorphous nonspecific groups, although, in the former case, at least two factions of Sendero Luminoso (Shining Path, or SL)— which fought a highly bloody civil war between 1980 and 1992[24]—

---

[20] Author interviews, Bogotá and Key West, March 2009.

[21] It should be noted that these cartels do not exist in the true economic sense of the word as they neither fix nor determine output and price.

[22] "The Colombian Cartels," *Frontline Drugwars*, undated; Mejia and Posada, 2008, p. 26; Saab and Taylor, 2009, pp. 465–466; United Nations Office on Drugs and Crime, *World Drug Report 2007*, 2007a.

[23] Author interviews, Cartagena, November 2008.

[24] SL emerged in 1980 with the stated aim of fomenting a cultural revolution to replace what it saw as Peru's bourgeois democracy with a "New Democracy" based on a proletariat dictatorship. For the next 12 years, the group waged a highly bloody civil war that was funded, in large part, by profits from the cocaine trade. In 1992, SL's leader Abimael Guzmán was captured, capping a largely successful (if extremely brutal and abusive) counterinsurgency campaign carried out by then-president Alberto Fujimori. Since then, the group has been

have resurfaced as increasingly prominent security subcontractors for local coca farmers.[25] Most indigenous activity revolves around local cultivation of fields, with actual processing and refining taking place in Brazil and, to a lesser extent, Argentina. Colombian and Mexican groups appear to dominate the latter effort, developing it as an integral component of their overall transatlantic narcotic export chain (see above).[26]

Mexico

Groups in Mexico constitute a critical component in the overall Latin American drug trade—dominating control of the actual movement of narcotics into mainland United States, as well as subsequent distribution in major metropolitan areas.[27] In this latter respect, they work closely with street gangs, which have established an especially strong influence in Los Angeles and the "tri-border" region of Washington, D.C., Maryland, and Virginia (discussed in more detail in Chapter Five). According to a 2008 assessment prepared by the U.S. Department of Justice, Mexican trafficking organizations have gained more control over the U.S. supply chain than any other ethnic criminal group (availed by the large expatriate community that exists across the country), yielding profit levels between $18 billion and $39 billion. A U.S. Justice Department report released in 2008 estimated that Mexican syndicates were now operating in all but two states (Vermont and West Virginia) and had a decisive presence in at least 195 major U.S.

---

only sporadically active, though it has never been fully eliminated as an entity in its own right. For more on the SL and the Peruvian state's response to its insurgency, see Charles Kenney, *Fujimori's Coup and the Breakdown of Democracy in Latin America*, Notre Dame, Ind.: University of Notre Dame Press, 2004; David Scott Palmer, ed., *The Shining Path of Peru*, New York: St. Martin's Press, 2nd ed., 1994; and Steve J. Stern, ed., *Shining and Other Paths: War and Society in Peru, 1980–1995*, Durham, N.C.: Duke University Press, 1998.

[25] Author interviews, Cartagena, November 2008. See also S. Romero, 2009a.

[26] Author interviews, Miami, Washington, D.C., Bogotá, and Key West, November 2008–March 2009.

[27] Author interviews, Washington, D.C., February 2009.

cities. Of these metropolitan hubs, Atlanta had been most-thoroughly penetrated, acting as a de facto clearinghouse for drug shipments to the Carolinas, Tennessee, the mid-Atlantic states, New York, and New England.[28]

Although President Calderón has decisively moved to dislodge the cartels' power base since taking office in 2006, several prominent organizations continue to exist largely due to pervasive corruption that has extended to the very highest echelons of the police and law enforcement bureaucracy (see below). Seven syndicates of varying strength have remained at the forefront of the trade:[29]

- Gulf cartel. For many years, the Gulf cartel was considered the most powerful of the Mexican syndicates, enforcing its control through a highly feared paramilitary arm known as Los Zetas. Since 2007, however, the dominance of the group has begun to wither—both as a result of a sustained counterdrug effort instituted by the Calderón administration and due to the defection of Los Zetas in January 2010, which now appears to act as an independent organization in its own right. At the time of this writing, much of the Gulf cartel's leadership structure had collapsed, further contributing to the group's organizational confusion and loss of direction.[30]

---

[28] See Francisco E. González, "Mexico's Drug Wars Get Brutal," *Current History*, Vol. 108, No. 715, February 2009, p. 76; Josh Meyer, "48 Arrested in U.S. Raid on Mexican Drug Cartel," *Los Angeles Times*, February 26, 2009; Moore, 2009; and Larry Copeland and Kevin Johnson, "Mexican Cartels Plague Atlanta," *USA Today*, March 9, 2009.

[29] Apart from the seven groups mentioned here, another syndicate emerged in 2008. Known as the Chiquilín Gang, it is essentially a creation of Manuel García Simental, a former enforcer in the Tijuana cartel known for his brutality and ruthlessness. However, the organization is only a relatively minor player and has been substantially weakened by the capture of its top leaders, including Simental (in December 2009) and his brother Raydel López Uriarte (a.k.a. El Muletas). At the time of this writing, the short to medium prospects of the gang were unclear. For further details, see "Mexico Arrests 2 Reputed Leaders of Tijuana Gang," Associated Press, February 8, 2010; and Marc Lacey, "Top Mexican Drug Suspect Arrested," *International Herald Tribune*, January 14, 2010a.

[30] Notable in this regard was the capture of the Gulf cartel's symbolic leader, Osiel Cárdenas, who was extradited to the United States in January 2007 (Fred Burton and Stephen

- La Familia Organization. La Familia emerged in 2006 with the purported dual aim of "defending citizens, merchants, businesses and farmers" from all forms of crime and filling the security void left by the central government. Since its creation, however, the organization has become systematically involved in drug trafficking, as well as money laundering and extortion.[31] The group has also become notorious for what it refers to as "social work"— endorsing the execution, by beheading, of those who do not conform to the parameters of its imposed "law enforcement" code.[32] At the time of this writing, La Familia had an estimated 4,000 members, with a confirmed presence in 77 cities across the states of Michoacán, Querétaro, Guanajuato, Jalisco, Colima, Aguascalientes, and Guerrero, as well as the federal district.[33]

- Los Zetas. As noted above, Los Zetas has emerged as an increasingly significant player for the trafficking of Latin American narcotics. The group was founded by former members of the Grupos Aeromóviles de Fuerzas (GAFE), an elite special forces unit, who deserted from the Mexican military between 1996 and 2000.[34] The organization is reportedly led by Heriberto "El Lazca" Lazcano and primarily operates out of Tamaulipas state, although, in recent years, it has expanded its presence to Veracruz,

---

Meiners, "Mexico and the War Against the Drug Cartels in 2008," *Global Security and Intelligence Report*, December 9, 2008; George Grayson, "Mexico and the Drug Cartels," Foreign Policy Research Institute, August 2007; Jo Tuckman, "Body Count Mounts as Drug Cartels Battle Each Other—and the Police," *Guardian* [UK], May 27, 2008a; "5630 Execution Murders in 2008: Mexican Drug Cartels," *Right Side News*, January 1, 2009).

[31] This evolution closely parallels that which occurred with the AUC in Colombia.

[32] Mexican authorities attributed no fewer than 17 decapitations to La Familia in 2006 alone.

[33] Oscar Becerra, "Family Business: La Familia: Mexico's Most Violent Criminals," *Jane's Intelligence Review*, October 7, 2009c, p. 41; George Grayson, "La Familia: Another Deadly Mexican Syndicate," Foreign Policy Research Institute, February 2009; Grayson, 2007.

[34] According to Mexican authorities, as many as 1,000 members of GAFE have deserted from the army since the late 1990s. Those critical to the formation of Los Zetas included Arturo Guzmán Decena (a.k.a. Z-1, now dead), Maximino Ortiz, Víctor Hernández Barron, Augustin Hernández Martínez, Juan Carlos Tovar, Pedro Cervantes Márquez, Ramiro Rangel, and Samuel Flores (all arrested).

Tabasco, Campeche, the capital territory, and Chiapas. Although Los Zetas' influence remains strong, its ability to consolidate control across the border provinces has been curtailed by the arrest of several top commanders during 2008. Four in particular were thought to have had a major impact: Mateo López (a.k.a. Comandante Mateo), Efraín Teodoro Torres (a.k.a. Z-14), Daniel Pérez Rojas (a.k.a. El Cachetes), and Jaime González Duran (a.k.a. El Hummer). The first three were all high-ranking members in the group's overall leadership structure, while the fourth was responsible for coordinating and overseeing cocaine imports from Central America.[35]

- Beltrán Leyva Organization. The Beltrán Leyva Organization was originally part of the Sinaloa Federation (see below) but broke from the latter in early 2008 after the group's leader (Alfredo Beltrán Leyva) was arrested following an alleged Sinaloan betrayal. The cartel has proven capable of resisting competition for territorial control from its former "parent" organization, as well as infiltrating counternarcotic units and assassinating some of their most-senior officers—including federal police director Edgar Millán Gómez (killed in May 2008).[36] Although the group remains prominent, its influence has withered due to the loss of some of its senior members, including, notably, the death of its then-current leader, Arturo Beltrán Leyva, in December 2009

---

[35] George Grayson, "Los Zetas: The Ruthless Army Spawned by a Mexican Drug Cartel," Foreign Policy Research Institute, May 2008; Oscar Becerra, "A to Z of Crime: Mexico's Zetas Expand Operations," *Jane's Intelligence Review*, January 27, 2009a, pp. 44–49; Burton and Meiners, 2008; Tuckman, 2008a; J. Sullivan and Elkus, 2008, p. 4; and "Small Arms Trafficking from the United States to Mexico," *Universal Adversary Special Analysis*, February 1, 2009, p. 8.

[36] Burton and Meiners, 2008; J. Sullivan and Elkus, 2008, p. 9; George Friedman, "Mexico: On the Road to a Failed State?" STRATFOR, May 13, 2008; Grayson, 2007; F. González, 2009, p. 75; James C. McKinley, "Gunmen Kill Chief of Mexico's Police," *New York Times*, May 9, 2008a; James C. McKinley, "6 Charged in Shooting of Officer in Mexico," *New York Times*, May 13, 2008b. In the United States, Gomez's rank was equivalent to that of the director of the Federal Bureau of Investigation (FBI).

and the subsequent arrest of his brother, Carlos Beltrán Leyva, in January 2010.[37]

- Sinaloa cartel. Despite the loss of key allies, including the Beltrán Leyva Organization and the Carrillo Fuentes syndicate, the Sinaloa cartel continues to be an active player on the Mexican narcotics scene. The group is led by Joaquín "El Chapo" Guzmán—the most-wanted drug lord in Mexico[38]—and counted among its membership the infamous Teodoro García Simental (a.k.a. El Teo, arrested in January 2010), who was believed to have been behind many of the intergang killings that plagued the border states during 2008.[39] Sinaloan distribution cells have been established throughout the United States and are now also appearing in Latin America to facilitate the transshipment of Peruvian and Colombian cocaine to West Africa and Europe.[40]
- Carrillo Fuentes syndicate (a.k.a. Juarez cartel). The Carrillo Fuentes syndicate is based in the northern city of Ciudad Juárez in Chihuahua state. The organization is led by Vicente Carrillo Fuentes, maintains an alliance with the Beltrán Leyva group, and is similarly fighting the Sinaloans for control of Juárez. At its height, the Carrillo Fuentes syndicate was assumed to be responsible for

---

[37] Lacey, 2010a; "Mexico Captures Brother of Slain Cartel Boss," Associated Press, January 3, 2010. Arturo Beltrán Leyva was killed by naval special forces; his brother was arrested carrying a false driver's license identifying him as Carlos Orpineda Gamez. A third member of the family, Mario, is still at large and is assumed to be the current leader of the organization.

[38] In 2009, Forbes magazine included Guzmán on its list of the world's richest men (701 out of 793) with an estimated fortune of $1 billion. See Randal C. Archibold, "Drug War in Mexico Pushes into US Homes," *International Herald Tribune*, March 24, 2009c.

[39] Richard Marosi and Ken Ellingwood, "Mexican Drug Lord Teodoro Garcia Simental, Known for His Savagery, Is Captured," *Los Angeles Times*, January 13, 2010. Simental's younger brother was arrested less than three week later, ending the spike in violence in Tijuana, where the two had operated. For further details on Simental's background, see Richard Marosi, "A City Goes Silent at His Name," *Los Angeles Times*, December 18, 2008, and Marc Lacey, "Mexican Man Admits Using Acid on Bodies, Army Says," *New York Times*, January 24, 2009a.

[40] Burton and Meiners, 2008; Grayson, 2007; Tuckman, 2008a; "5630 Execution Murders in 2008," 2009.

about half of all the illegal drugs that pass through Mexico to the United States, with some U.S. sources estimating its income as high as $200 million per week.[41] Although the Beltrán Leyva has systematically eclipsed the group's activities, its members continue to retain a reputation for extreme violence and, indeed, were implicated in the infamous Cuidad Juárez serial-murder site that was first reported in 2004 and that has since been dubbed the House of Death.[42]

- Arellano Félix organization (a.k.a. Tijuana cartel). The Arellano Félix organization, which operates across northwestern Mexico, was at one time dubbed one of the biggest and most-violent crime families in the country.[43] However, in recent years, the cartel has been weakened almost beyond recognition as a result of the arrest or elimination of several of its highest-ranking leaders. These have included, notably, Benjamin Arellano Félix, Carlos Arellano Félix, Eduardo Arellano, Ramón Eduardo Arellano Félix, and Francisco Javier Arellano Félix. These losses have decisively curtailed the cartel's penetration and reach, with competitors, such as the Sinaloa federation, increasingly muscling into the organization's home turf and taking control of some of its key smuggling routes.[44]

These various groups can essentially be spilt into two main competing blocs: the Sinaloa federation, Gulf cartel, and La Familia, which,

---

[41] Burton and Meiners, 2008; Howard LaFranchi, "A Look Inside a Giant Drug Cartel," *Christian Science Monitor*, December 6, 1999.

[42] See David Rose, "House of Death," *Observer* (UK), December 3, 2006; Alfredo Corchado, "Drug Wars' Long Shadow," *Dallas Morning News*, December 13, 2008; and Radley Balko, "The House of Death," *Reason*, September 30, 2008.

[43] Tim Steller, "Mexican Drug Runners May Have Used C-130 from Arizona," *Arizona Daily Star*, April 15, 1998.

[44] Burton and Meiners, 2008; Elizabeth Diaz, "Analysis: Mexico's Tijuana Cartel Weaker as Ex-Boss Comes Home," Reuters, March 14, 2008; Tuckman, 2008a; "Mexican Drug Lord Is Arrested," Reuters, October 26, 2008. At the time of this writing, Enedina Arellano Félix, one of four sisters, was acting as the group's ostensible leader, managing most of its organized-crime and money-laundering operations.

in February 2010, formed the New Federation; and a loose pattern of shifting alliances among the remaining five syndicates. This alliance structure appears to have some longevity built into it, given bonds of mutually beneficial business relationships and, just as importantly, vendettas and unpaid blood debts.

Africa and Europe

Beyond Central and Latin America, two other major entities play an important role in the trafficking of Andean cocaine. First are West African syndicates, particularly those based in Ghana and Guinea-Bissau. These polycentric groups collectively number several thousand members and constitute the main vehicle by which Colombian, Peruvian, and Bolivian cocaine is (indirectly) shipped to Western Europe. Drugs are generally moved overland to the Maghreb and then sent across the Mediterranean using established hashish routes that run from Morocco, Algeria, and Tunisia.[45]

Occasionally, air couriers will be recruited to fly either directly or indirectly into major consumption cities, such as London, Rome, Paris, Amsterdam, Milan, Madrid, and Berlin.[46] The mean pay for these "human mules" is US$3,000–$5,000 per trip, plus expenses— which is substantially more than an average West African is likely to earn in a year and, therefore, ensures a ready supply of willing accomplices. Smuggling techniques for air couriers vary from the use of simple strap-on body packs to the ingestion of small drug-filled bags, which have numbered as many as 90 in a single person. More-effective European drug interdiction has also prompted West African groups to recruit traffickers that are less likely to attract the attention of inspecting custom authorities, including women, the elderly, westerners, the handicapped (one heroin ring in Lagos became especially adept at

---

[45] Author interviews, Washington, D.C., January and February 2009.

[46] Couriers generally fly from Nigeria, Senegal, Guinea, or Mali, transiting countries in North Africa and southern Europe. See Webb-Vidal, 2009a, p. 48.

hiding opiates in wheelchairs), college students, and, allegedly, even children.[47]

Second is the Calabrian 'Ndrangheta, a principal mafia in Italy and the one with the greatest international reach. The organization has a cell-based structure that has proven largely immune from insider betrayals due to the strong family ties that underscore its wider structure.[48] According to a 2008 report by the Istituto di Studi Politici, Economici e Sociali (EURISPES) social studies group, this effective self-insulation from police informants, together with its ready access to facilities across Italy, the Netherlands, Spain, and Belgium, is one of the principal factors that has encouraged Colombian syndicates to work with the 'Ndrangehta in arranging and facilitating the final distribution of drugs in Europe. A major counternarcotics operation in 2007, Stupor Mundi, revealed that the 'Ndrangheta was capable of purchasing and moving up to 3 tons of Colombian cocaine at a time—with a street value of roughly €60 million (approximately US$74.5 million)—graphically underscoring the extensive scope of this bilateral "business collaboration."[49] Unlike West African syndicates, the 'Ndrangheta has managed to establish its own presence in Latin America, particularly Brazil, suggesting that it might now be moving to consolidate a greater role in the Latin American transatlantic drug supply chain, at least with respect to coca originally cultivated in Peru and Bolivia.

---

[47] See, for instance, Peter Chalk, *Non-Military Security and Global Order: The Impact of Extremism, Violence and Chaos on National and International Stability*, London: Macmillan, 2000, p. 44; Webb-Vidal, 2009a; "Drugs Courier Dies After Swallowing 500g of Cocaine," *Independent* (UK), November 10, 1992.

[48] Italian authorities believe that there are approximately 131 separate 'Ndrangheta families (or 'ndrine) active in the greater Calabrian region. One of the largest, based in Gioia Tauro, numbers approximately 400 members with several thousand affiliates.

[49] Michele Brunelli, "The Italian Connection: Calabrian Mafia's Power Base Has Expanded," *Jane's Intelligence Review*, December 2008, pp. 38–43.

CHAPTER FOUR

Trafficking Vessels

More than 80 percent of the cocaine that arrives in the United States, either directly or via Mexico, is shipped from Latin America by means of noncommercial maritime conveyance.[1] Three main vessels currently predominate the eastern Pacific and Caribbean corridors that make up this route: fishing trawlers, go-fasts, and self-propelled semisubmersibles (SPSSs).

Fishing Trawlers

Up until 2006, most Latin American cocaine and heroin was moved direct to Mexico in single consignments. Deepwater fishing trawlers were the favored vessels for these shipments, not least because of their sophisticated navigation and communication technologies. In most cases, drugs would be concealed in legitimate cargo, packed in metal containers welded to the ship's hull, hidden in false bulkheads, or stored in secret engine compartments.[2] Traffickers also toyed with liquefying cocaine so that it could be stored in fuel and ballast tanks

---

[1] Author interviews, Washington, D.C., February 2009, and Bogotá, March 2009. The remaining 20 percent is sent by air. Flights (narcos avionetas) generally originate from Venezuela or Brazil, where numerous clandestine runways exist. Drugs are mostly shipped in light-wing planes that are capable of carrying a payload between 3 and 5 metric tons. It should also be noted that, although maritime conveyance dominates, drugs are often offloaded in Central America and therefore have to be trafficked overland north to Mexico and subsequently to the United States.

[2] Author interviews, Bogotá, March 2009.

but apparently abandoned this method due to the high costs associated with the reprocessing of the drug.[3]

Although fishing trawlers are still periodically used for drug runs, Latin American syndicates have progressively moved away from shipping large volumes via direct routes due to more-effective interdiction in the eastern Pacific.[4] As noted below, the preferred method today is to spread risk by smuggling smaller but more-numerous volumes in go-fasts. That said, trawlers still play a role in trafficking operations by acting as "scouts" for active drug boats or refueling platforms for semi-submersibles undertaking long-haul trips.[5]

Go-Fasts

Since 2006, Latin American syndicates have attempted to inoculate the integrity of their cocaine shipments by adopting a "scatter gun" approach to surface-water trafficking. Rather than moving concentrated consignments in solo runs, loads are now dispersed and smuggled in stages. The new stratagem is designed to maximize the security for each payload, both by shortening the response time available to interception craft and by reducing the statistical probability of losing the entire cargo to one dedicated seizure.[6]

The typical boat used for these types of shipments is the go-fast. Constructed out of wood that is then covered by fiberglass, these vessels are capable of carrying up to 2 MT of drugs at a time. Go-fasts lie low in the water and are powered by four 200hp Yamaha outboard

---

[3] Author interviews, Cartagena, November 2008, and Washington, D.C., February 2009.

[4] To a large degree, more-effective interdiction reflects an accord that sanctions the U.S. Coast Guard (USCG) with the authority to interdict and impound any Colombian vessel suspected of smuggling drugs that is sailing beyond Bogotá's 12-mile territorial limit. Although the right to board is not automatic—requiring approval from Colombia—this is a formality and is usually granted within 30 minutes by fax (author interview, Washington, D.C., February 2009).

[5] Author interviews, Washington, D.C., January and February 2009, and Key West, March 2009.

[6] Author interviews, Cartagena, November 2008.

engines that give them a top speed approaching 70mph (which is far quicker than the antiquated interdiction craft of Central American and Caribbean navies). They are typically painted a dark color or covered with aquamarine tarps to disguise their configuration and frequently escape radar detection. In one case that occurred in the summer of 2008, for instance, a UK and two U.S. coast guard cutters failed to detect a go-fast that was lying stationary between them, even though they had the coordinates of its position and were separated by just half a mile. In that event, the vessel was spotted only when the airflow from a low-flying surveillance plane disturbed the tarpaulin that was draped over the boat.[7]

Go-fasts will "hop-scotch" up the Central American/eastern Caribbean coast, hugging the shoreline and mixing with legitimate littoral traffic to avoid patrols by the USCG and international navies. According to U.S. sources, go-fasts account for more than 50 percent of all current drug movements out of Colombia and will, in all likelihood, continue to be a favored means for transporting cocaine over the short to medium term.[8]

Self-Propelled Semisubmersibles

Apart from surface boats, Colombian syndicates also use SPSSs. These vessels are principally employed for large drug runs in the eastern Pacific and can carry loads of between 6 and 10 MT, although most operate at around 75-percent capacity.[9] The standard range for a semi is between 500 and 1,000 nm. However, some have been purpose-built to reach distances upward of 1,500 nm, which puts them well within the vicinity of Mexican waters. If a voyage of this distance is to

---

[7] Author interviews, Cartagena, November 2008, and Washington, D.C., February 2009; U.S. Department of State, *International Narcotics Control Strategy Report*, Washington, D.C., 2007.

[8] Author interviews, Cartagena, November 2008, Washington, D.C., February 2009, and Bogotá, March 2009.

[9] SPSSs' lack of buoyancy means that they can operate at only 75-percent capacity if stability and ballast are to be ensured (author interview, Bogotá, March 2009).

be made, the SPSS will usually depart from southern Colombia, travel due west to the Galapagos Islands, and then turn north, typically rendezvousing with a fishing trawler at a preassigned location to take on additional fuel. A semi undertaking one of these trips was apprehended in July 2008 with more than 6 MT of cocaine onboard.[10]

SPSSs are generally constructed from scratch in jungle boatyards within 30 to 40 miles from the northern coastal city of Barranquilla; officials with Washington's Joint Interagency Task Force–South (JIATF-S) estimate that between 50 and 80 vessels are produced each year at a unit cost of $1 million to $2 million. A standard semi is constructed out of wood overlaid with roughly 25 tons of fiberglass and equipped with 5 tons of lead ballast, one to two diesel engines, air-intake valves, and electronic navigation systems. Fifty-four of these craft have been seized since 1993, with 20 captured in 2009 alone.[11] SPSSs are designed to sit several meters below the sea's surface with only the coning tower exposed above the waterline (generally about a foot or so). However, in 2010, DEA reportedly seized a fully functional, completely submersible vessel that authorities believe had been constructed for transoceanic voyages. If verified, this would mark a "quantum leap" in drug-smuggling evasion technology.[12]

SPSSs are usually crewed by four to six persons and can be used for single or multiple journeys. In the latter case, the rudder and propeller shaft are covered in zinc to protect against corrosion. They emit

---

[10] Author interviews, Washington, D.C., February 2009, and Key West, March 2009. See also "Mexico: Cocaine Found in Small Sub," Reuters, July 19, 2008.

[11] Author interviews, Cartagena, November 2008, and Bogotá, March 2009. See also "Colombian Navy Destroys Drug Sub," Latin American Herald Tribune, February 24, 2010; McDermott, 2010, p. 44; Christian Le Miere, "Insurgent Submersibles," Jane's Terrorism and Security Monitor, June 16, 2008; and "Narco Subs: New Challenge in the Drug War," Dialogo, Vol. 18, No. 4, 2008, pp. 34–35.

[12] Frank Bajak, "DEA: Seized Submarine Quantum Leap for Narcos," Associated Press, July 4, 2010.

no radar trace and effectively eliminate infrared signatures by dissipat-ing engine heat through keel coolers.[13]

Most SPSSs are equipped with a scuttling valve, which is designed to rapidly sink the ship in the event that it is spotted by a coastal patrol boat. As the vessel goes down—a process that generally takes little more than 12 minutes—the traffickers jump overboard, forcing the interdiction team to perform an immediate search-and-rescue mission (which they are obliged to do under international law). By the time this is completed, the semi, together with its incriminating cargo, is, in all probability, lost, leaving the authorities little option but to release any apprehended crew. In an effort to overcome this particular problem, the U.S. government passed legislation in November 2008 (in congru-ence with the Colombian National Parliament) making it a criminal offense to operate a semisubmersible, irrespective of whether evidence existed that the vessel was being used to transship narcotics.[14]

---

[13] Author interviews, Cartagena, November 2008, and Bogotá, March 2009. Zinc erodes more quickly than metal, so the blocs essentially sacrifice themselves to protect the compo-nent structures to which they are attached.

[14] Author interviews, Cartagena, November 2008, and Key West, March 2009.

CHAPTER FIVE

Impact

South America and Central America

The Latin American drug trade has had a pervasive and insidious impact that has affected a wide spectrum of national, regional, and even international security interests. In Colombia, revenue from the production and trafficking of heroin and cocaine has provided FARC with sufficient operational capital to maintain an active war footing in its ongoing conflict against Bogotá. Although the organization does not pose a strategic threat to the central government, its activities have undermined popular confidence in the administration's ability to project a concerted territorial presence, guarantee public security, and maintain a (legitimate) monopoly of violence—all key components of sovereign statehood. There is little question that, without access to the enormous profits availed by the drug trade, FARC's ability to "achieve" these debilitating effects would have been greatly curtailed.[1]

Compounding the situation in Colombia are the activities of reemerging paramilitary gangs. In particular, fighting and competition between these groups has contributed to an increasingly serious humanitarian crisis. According to the United Nations High Commissioner for Refugees (UNHCR), 27,000 internal refugees were registered in the state during 2008, more than double the figure for 2007.[2]

---

[1] Author interview, Miami, November 2008.

[2] Kraul, 2008c; Kraul, 2008b.

These numbers make up a major proportion of the overall national displacement picture, which currently remains among the world's worst.[3]

Beyond Colombia, the drug trade is helping to reenergize the SL guerrilla war in Peru, which supposedly ended in 2000. According to analysts with the Catholic University in Lima, at least two factions of the organization are currently seeking to entrench themselves in the country's cocaine trade by acting as security subcontractors for indigenous farmers.[4] These blocs allegedly employ about 350 combatants to protect farmers and their fields and, in 2008, were linked to the deaths of at least 26 people (including 22 soldiers and police), making it the bloodiest year in almost a decade. As Antezana of the Catholic University remarks, "the guerrillas are now able to operate with the efficiency and deadliness of an elite drug trafficking organization."[5]

Elsewhere, the cocaine trade is feeding a growing addiction problem. In 2008, an estimated 2.7 million people were using cocaine in South and Central America and the Caribbean, accounting for about 20 percent of global consumption.[6] Indeed, according to Caribbean security officials, countries, such as Puerto Rico and the Dominican Republic, are now as much consumption states as they are transit hubs. The resulting strain on the public health system has been significant—the Santo Domingo government in the Dominican Republic is reportedly devoid of the necessary assets required to treat the rapidly escalating number of addicts in the country—as has been the knock-on effect on inner-city violence with gangs increasingly competing with one another for control of lucrative sales turf.[7]

---

[3] Chaskel and Bustamante, 2008, p. 79; Simon Romero, "Wider Drug War Threatens Colombian Indians," *New York Times*, April 21, 2009b. At the time of this writing, Colombia had about 3 million internal refugees, although, during the past two decades, more than 20 million people are estimated to have been forced to flee their homes as a result of threats of aggression and acts of violence from left-wing guerrillas and paramilitaries.

[4] S. Romero, 2009a.

[5] Cited in S. Romero, 2009a.

[6] UNODC, 2010, p. 71.

[7] Author interviews, Cartagena, November 2008. See also United Nations High Commissioner for Refugees, "Freedom in the World 2008: Dominican Republic," *Refworld*, July 2, 2008.

It is in Mexico, however, that the pernicious societal impact of the Latin American cocaine and heroin trade has been greatest, contributing to what amounts to the wholesale breakdown of basic civility across the country—something that has been particularly evident in the northern border states.[8] According to Guillermo Valdés Castellanos, director of the National Security and Intelligence Center (Centro de Investigación y Seguridad Nacional, or CISEN), more than 28,000 drug-related murders have occurred since Felipe Calderón launched an all-out offensive on the country's cartels in 2006.[9] To put these figures in perspective, note that fewer than 4,300 U.S. soldiers lost their lives in Iraq between 2003 and 2008. The enormous human toll has triggered the formation of various self-defense forces across the border provinces. In January 2009, for instance, a group calling itself the Juárez Citizens Command announced that it was preparing to take the law into its own hands and would execute a criminal every 24 hours to bring order to the city.[10]

Most killings are the work of syndicate-controlled paramilitary cells, some with professional training. Notable groups include Los Negros, Los Gueritos, Los Pelones, Los Números, Los Chachos, Los Lobos, Los Sinaloa, and Los Nuevos Zetas.[11] Ensuing fatalities have been linked to intersyndicate warfare, the silencing of suspected informers, the assassination of high-ranking officials, and the systematic targeting of law enforcement personnel. The latter has become

---

[8] Although most focus is on violence in the northern border states, it is important to note that the breakdown in civility is occurring around the country, including Sinaloa (Culiacán); Guerrero (Acapulco); Michoacán (Morelia); Morelos (Cuernavaca); and Durango, Torreón, and Jalisco (Guadalajara), to name just a few places. The Trans-Border Institute at the University of San Diego has published detailed analyses on the social and civil impact of the drug trade in Mexico. Papers, research briefs, and fact sheets can be accessed online (Trans-Border Institute, "Border Resources," undated web page). See also Bernard Debusmann, "Among Top US Fears: A Failed Mexico State," *International Herald Tribune*, January 10, 2009.

[9] David Agren, "Mexico: Death Toll from Drug-Related Violence Is Thousands Higher Than Was Reported Earlier," *New York Times*, August 3, 2010.

[10] Robert Munks, "Mexico Murders Presage More Violence," *Jane's Intelligence Review*, February 2010, p. 1.

[11] See "Small Arms Trafficking from the United States to Mexico," 2009, p. 12.

increasingly evident in line with Calderón's antidrug push since 2006. In many cases, police either quit (certain towns have seen entire forces abandon the job) or cooperate with syndicates out of straight fear. Although it is lower- and mid-ranking officers who have been mostly affected, traffickers have been prepared to direct their intimidation to the highest levels. In 2009, for instance, the police chief of Cuidad Juárez, Roberto Orduña Cruz, fled the city after his deputy, operations director Sacramento Pérez Serrano, was shot. The assassination was in keeping with a cartel ultimatum that a senior official would be killed every 48 hours until he resigned.[12]

The specific character of drug-related murders has also become progressively more barbaric. It is not unusual for victims to be dismembered, beheaded, boiled in giant pots filled with lye (a process known as pozole after the Mexican word for stew), or even skinned.[13] As one official in Tijuana candidly remarked,

> Criminals earn respect and credibility with creative killing methods. Your status is based on your capacity to commit the most sadistic acts. Burning corpses, using acid, beheading victims. . . . This generation is setting a new standard for savagery.[14]

The extent of cartel violence has begun to take on a disturbing new dimension with the deliberate targeting of ordinary civilians. A particularly bloody attack took place in September 2008, when two fragmentation grenades were hurled into a crowd celebrating Mexico's Independence Day at the Plaza Melchor Ocampo in Morelia, Michoacán state. The atrocity, which was originally blamed on La Familia but ultimately tied to Los Zetas, resulted in eight deaths and more than

---

[12] See F. González, 2009, p. 75; Marc Lacey, "With Force Mexican Drug Cartels Get Their Way," *New York Times*, February 28, 2009b; J. Sullivan and Elkus, 2008, p. 4; and "Mexico Town's Entire Police Force Quits in Fear of Assassination," Associated Press, May 23, 2008.

[13] See, for instance, Lacey, 2010a; Ken Ellingwood, "Extreme Drug Violence Grips Mexico Border City," *Los Angeles Times*, December 19, 2008; F. González, 2009, p. 72; James C. McKinley, "Two Sides of a Border: One Violent, One Peaceful," *New York Times*, January 22, 2009; Tuckman, 2008a; and Lacey, 2009a.

[14] Cited in Marosi, 2008.

100 injuries.[15] Commenting on the incident and what it might herald, Jane's Homeland Security Review remarks,

> [The Morelia bombing] indicated that there is a disturbing evolution towards indiscriminate attacks on a large-scale using a methodology . . . which seems to be inspired more by terrorist techniques than by traditional cartel activity. . . . A new chapter in Mexico's drugs war has now opened and future attacks on this scale must now be considered a reality of security risk.[16]

This assessment was borne out in February 2010, when drug traffickers stormed a party packed with teenagers in Cuidad Juárez and indiscriminately killed 14 people, eight of whom were under 20. According to the daily El Diario, one of the victims had been a witness to a multiple homicide and was due to have testified in an upcoming trial.[17]

Apart from fostering extreme violence, the narcotics trade has decisively undermined political stability in Mexico by feeding pervasive corruption throughout the police and administrative bureaucracy.[18] Although the overall extent of the problem is unknown, its seriousness can be gauged by the following statistics:

---

[15] Burton and Meiners, 2008; Grayson, 2009; F. González, 2009, p. 72; Marc Lacey, "Blasts Kill 7 at Celebration in Mexican President's Hometown," *New York Times*, September 16, 2008a; Miguel Garcia, "Grenade Attacks Kill 8 on Mexico's National Day," Reuters, September 16, 2008; Jo Tuckman, "Revellers Killed in Grenade Attack on Mexican Independence Celebrations," *Guardian* (UK), September 16, 2008b.

[16] "Securing America's Borders," *Jane's Homeland Security Review*, February 2009, p. 26. The Jane's article makes the additional point that, although future attacks against civilians are likely, the widespread use of this tactic is mitigated by the instability that it engenders and the associated weakening of state structures on which cartels paradoxically depend to survive.

[17] Ken Ellingwood, "As Mexican Teens Celebrate School Soccer Win, Gunmen Open Fire," *Los Angeles Times*, February 1, 2010.

[18] For an overview of the extent of narcotics-related corruption in Mexico, see Laurie Freeman, *State of Siege: Drug-Related Violence and Corruption in Mexico*, Washington, D.C.: Washington Office on Latin America, June 2006.

- One-fifth of Mexico's entire federal police force was under investigation for corruption as of 2005.[19]
- Between 2006 and 2008, 11,500 public servants were fined or suspended from their jobs for corruption.[20]
- In April 2007, the Monterrey state government arrested an unprecedented 141 police officers for collaborating with the Gulf cartel and accepting kickbacks in exchange for intelligence or ignoring trafficking activities taking place in their respective jurisdictions.[21]
- In 2008, more than 35 high-ranking security officials were detained, notably including Noe Ramírez, a former head of the anti–organized crime unit in the attorney general's office, and Ricardo Gutiérrez Vargas, director for International Police Affairs at the Federal Investigative Agency (FIA).[22]
- In 2010, nearly one-tenth of the officers in the federal police force were dismissed for failing to pass anticorruption tests.[23]

Evidence suggests that corruption among police and immigration officials who are stationed in the northern border provinces is especially acute where many are offered cash payments to cooperate with drug syndicates and threatened with physical harm if bribes are not accept-

---

[19] James Verini, "Arming the Drug Wars," *Portfolio*, June 16, 2008; Manuel Roig-Franzia, "U.S. Guns Behind Cartel Killings in Mexico," *Washington Post*, October 29, 2007.

[20] Mario Gonzalez, "Mexico's Corruption Fight Reaches Civil Workers," *CNN.com*, December 9, 2008.

[21] Robin Emmott, "Police Corruption Undermines Mexico's War on Drugs," Reuters, May 23, 2007; "In Anti-Drug Move, Mexico Purges Police," *Los Angeles Times*, June 25, 2007.

[22] Elisabeth Malkin, "Mexico Arrests Ex-Chief of Antidrug Agency, *New York Times*, November 21, 2008; "In Drug Inquiry, Mexico Arrests Another Top Police Official," Associated Press, November 18, 2008; "Ex–Crime Chief Arrested in Mexico," *BBC News*, November 21, 2008; John P. Sullivan, "Outside View: Mexico's Criminal Insurgency," United Press International, December 18, 2008b. Ramírez and Vargas were both arrested on charges that they had received payments from various drug cartels in exchange for intelligence.

[23] Randal C. Archibold, "Mexican Leader Pushes Police Overhaul," *New York Times*, October 7, 2010b.

ed.[24] This method, known as plata o plomo ("silver or lead"), has been used repeatedly to avail cocaine and heroin (as well as marijuana)[25] shipments into the United States, casting considerable doubt on the overall veracity and credibility of the counterdrug offensive that was initiated in 2006.[26]

In an attempt to address this situation, the Calderón administration submitted a bill to the Mexican Congress in October 2010 that, if passed, would effectively phase out municipal police forces, which are deemed as being the most vulnerable to co-option and the ones most-frequently subjected to intimidation.[27] Under the plan, known as mando único (unified command), responsibility for local security would fall to state police, which would be controlled by governors and work closely with federal law enforcement.[28] The reform is designed to weed out corrupt officers, improve recruitment standards, and enhance training. Although Calderón has hailed the reform as one of the most-significant institutional changes of his presidency, others have questioned the initiative, noting that it neither alters how policing is actually carried out (merely changing who performs the function) nor takes

---

[24] "Small Arms Trafficking from the United States to Mexico," 2009, p. 11; Julia Preston, "Officers Team Up to Quell Violence," *New York Times*, March 26, 2010.

[25] Apart from cocaine and heroin, Mexican syndicates are also known to earn considerable profits from trafficking marijuana into the United States. In 2006, the Office of National Drug Control Policy (ONDCP) estimated that 60 percent of all income accruing to illegal drug groups in the country derived from marijuana exports. See George W. Bush, *National Drug Control Strategy 2006 Annual Report*, Washington, D.C., 2006.

[26] Author interviews, Cartagena, November 2008. See also "Small Arms Trafficking from the United States to Mexico," 2009; F. González, 2009, p. 75; Meyer, 2009; "Mexico's Drug Wars," *Financial Times* (UK), November 26, 2008; Marc Lacey, "Officials Say Drug Cartels Infiltrated Mexican Law Unit," *New York Times*, October 27, 2008b; Sara Miller Llana, "Setbacks in Mexico's War on Corruption," *Christian Science Monitor*, December 30, 2008.

[27] Although the plan has yet to be approved by the Mexican Congress, the state of Aguascalientes has unilaterally decided to implement the project within its own jurisdiction. See Ángel Álvarez, "Capital de Aguascalientes se une a Mando Único Policial," *La Crónica de Hoy*, October 12, 2008.

[28] Only municipal forces that satisfy stringent standards will remain intact, but, even then, they would be part of the state command.

account of the widespread problems that exist in both state and federal forces (as outlined above).[29]

The United States

Many of the negative impacts outlined above have relevance to the United States. Americans currently consume roughly 44 percent of the global cocaine supply, making the country the main market for Latin American cartels.[30] The sale, distribution, and use of narcotics in the United States has contributed to addiction and public health problems,[31] further exacerbated the breakdown of social and family relations, undermined economic productivity, and fueled street violence in prominent end-user cities, such as Los Angeles, Phoenix, Chicago, Denver, San Diego, Houston, Seattle, and San Francisco.[32] As the National Drug Intelligence Center within the U.S. Department of Justice observes,

> The trafficking and abuse of drugs in the United States affect nearly all aspects of our lives. . . . The damage caused by drug abuse and addiction is reflected in an overburdened justice system, a strained healthcare system, lost productivity and environmental destruction.[33]

---

[29] Archibold, 2010b. For a good overview of mando único and other police reform initiatives in Mexico, see Daniel Sabet, *Police Reform in Mexico: Advances and Persistent Obstacles*, Wilson Center, undated.

[30] Again, these entities do not act as cartels in the true economic sense of the word because they neither fix nor determine price or output.

[31] According to ONDCP, there are approximately 1.6 million hard-core cocaine addicts in the United States. See Office of National Drug Control Policy, *The President's National Drug Control Policy*, Washington, D.C., January 2009.

[32] Author interviews, Miami, November 2008.

[33] National Drug Intelligence Center, *National Drug Threat Assessment 2010*, Washington, D.C., February 2010, p. 3.

The narcotics trade has also significantly impeded fiscal growth and stability by diverting scarce resources away from more-productive uses. Between 1981 and 2008, federal, state, and local governments are estimated to have spent at least $600 billion (adjusted for inflation) on drug interdiction and related law enforcement efforts; factoring in costs associated with treatment and rehabilitation, the overall total rises to around $800 billion.[34] If one were to also add in "invisible" losses brought about by curtailed job opportunities and reduced workplace productivity, the true cost would be far higher. As ONDCP has observed, this financial burden is one that is shared by all of society, either directly or indirectly through higher tax dollars.[35]

Although not as pervasive as in other countries, corruption has been an additional problem confronting the United States. During a congressional hearing in March 2010, representatives from the FBI and the U.S. Department of Homeland Security (DHS) painted a disturbing picture of increased drug-syndicate infiltration into the ranks of the more than 41,000 frontline agents and officers who are now deployed along the U.S.-Mexico border.[36] One factor that has significantly availed this criminal penetration is a lack of appropriate vet-

---

[34] John Walsh, senior associate, Washington Office on Latin America, "U.S. Drug Policy: At What Cost? Moving Beyond the Self-Defeating Supply-Control Fixation," statement at "Illegal Drugs: Economic Impact, Societal Costs, Policy Responses," hearing of the U.S. Congress Joint Economic Committee, June 19, 2008. In 2008 alone, Washington spent $7 billion on drug-related law enforcement and interdiction efforts, in addition to another $5 billion on education, prevention, and treatment programs to curtail substance abuse ("Not Winning the War on Drugs," *New York Times*, July 2, 2008).

[35] George W. Bush, *National Drug Control Strategy 2008 Annual Report: Message from the President of the United States Transmitting the Administration's 2008 National Drug Control Strategy, Pursuant to 21 U.S.C. 1504*, Washington, D.C., 2008.

[36] In August 2010, for example, a female Customs and Border Patrol (CBP) officer was sentenced to 20 years in prison for helping to move significant quantities of cocaine from Cuidad Juárez into El Paso. The agent, Martha Garnica, had led a double life for many years and had devised secret codes and routes for smugglers to safely haul drugs (and undocumented workers) across the New Mexico border. She was, in the words of prosecutors, a "valued asset" of crime syndicates in Juárez, directing the movements of at least five men, four of whom have since been captured or killed. See Ceci Connolly, "Woman's Links to Mexican Drug Cartel a Saga of Corruption on U.S. Side of Border," *Washington Post*, September 12, 2010.

ting. Indeed, in 2009, 85 percent of new recruits received no polygraph examination, which experts believe to be one of the most-effective tools for identifying and weeding out bad hires. When asked to comment on this state of affairs and the potential number of border officials who might now be in place but susceptible to co-option, the chair of the March meeting, Senator Mark Pryor, pointedly described a situation that he believed to be both "alarming" and "dangerous."[37]

Beyond these effects, the Latin American narcotics trade is pertinent to U.S. national security interests because of its actual or potential negative interaction with other transnational challenges and potential threat contingencies. A direct correlation exists between the illicit trafficking of U.S.-made arms and current bouts of drug-related violence. According to the Brookings Institution, approximately 2,000 guns per day illegally cross into Mexico (where, due to stipulations imposed by the federal law on firearms and explosives, legitimately purchasing high-powered weapons is virtually impossible),[38] while a report by the Bureau of Alcohol, Tobacco, Firearms and Explosives estimated that more than 7,700 weapons bought in the United States eventually found their way south of the border.[39] These munitions are thought to account for roughly 90 percent of the weapons currently used by syndicates operating in Baja California, Chihuahua, Sonora, and Sinaloa.[40]

---

[37] Randal C. Archibold, "U.S. Falters in Screening Border Patrol Near Mexico," *New York Times*, March 11, 2010a. See also Connolly, 2010.

[38] For more on the law and its provisions, see "Small Arms Trafficking from the United States to Mexico," 2009, p. 3. See also "Mexico's Gun Laws for Americans," *Panda Programming*, last updated June 2, 2010; and Alfonso Serrano, "U.S.-Bought Guns Killing Mexican Police," *CBS News*, August 16, 2007.

[39] See Tracy Wilkinson, "U.S. War on Drugs Has Failed, Report Says," *Los Angeles Times*, November 27, 2008; Jeremy Binnie and Christian Le Miere, "In the Line of Fire," *Jane's Intelligence Review*, January 2009, p. 11; Randal C. Archibold, "Wave of Drug Violence Is Creeping into Arizona from Mexico, Officials Say," *New York Times*, February 23, 2009b; J. Sullivan and Elkus, 2008, p. 5; Roig-Franzia, 2007; F. González, 2009, p. 76; "Small Arms Trafficking from the United States to Mexico," 2009, p. 1; and Jacques Billeaud, "Cartels in Mexico's Drug War Get Guns from US," Associated Press, January 28, 2009.

[40] Author interviews, Miami, November 2008, and Phoenix, March 2009. See also Catherine Dooley and Ariadne Medler, "A Farewell to Arms: Managing Cross-Border Weapons Trafficking," *Hemisphere Focus*, Vol. XVI, No. 2, September 9, 2008; "Mexico's Attorney

Weapons are primarily procured with legitimate documentation at weekly gun shows in Texas, Arizona, and California, and then systematically smuggled to Mexican syndicates based across the southern U.S. border (a procedure known as straw purchases). Couriers typically transport a consignment of up to five weapons at a time that are either hidden in a false compartment of a vehicle or carried on their person if traveling by foot. Because of the sheer volume of people crossing the U.S.-Mexico border each day, the options for comprehensive searches are extremely limited. This ensures a slow but steady flow of munitions to drug cartels in what is now euphemistically referred to as "ant trafficking."[41] Routes follow one of four corridors: Gulf, Pacific, Central, and Southern.[42] Table 5.1 details the entry points for each of these conduits, as well as the location of onward destinations.

Assault rifles, machine guns, and high-caliber pistols constitute the most–frequently purchased arms, although heavier weaponry can also be obtained—much of it at comparatively low prices (see Tables 5.2 and 5.3). Not only is the ready availability of these munitions allowing cocaine smugglers to operate on a higher and more-lethal plane in Mexico; there are also growing indications that their violent activities are increasingly spilling over into or near southern U.S. border states. In March 2010, Leslie Enriquez, a U.S. consulate worker, was fatally

---

General Calls on US to Stop Guns, Drug Money," Associated Press, March 29, 2007; Douglass K. Daniel, "Gates: US Military Can Help Mexico in Drug Fight," Associated Press, March 2, 2009; "Mexico Corruption, U.S. Weapons Deepen Drug War Toll," *newsdesk.org*, April 5, 2007; and Donna Leinwand, "Authorities Try to Keep Guns from Drug Cartels," *USA Today*, December 10, 2008. It should be noted that Mexican syndicates also procure weapons from other sources, notably the Central American states of Honduras, Guatemala, and El Salvador. All of these countries are awash in arms (reflected in the extremely high murder rates that they all share) as a result of stocks left over from conflicts during the Cold War, many of which make their way north. Since 2006, for instance, at least 70,000 weapons from Guatemala have been seized in Mexico. See Andrew Eller, "Mexico's Other Border: Immigration and Drugs Along the Mexican/Guatemala Frontier," *HispanicVista*, undated web page; "Honduras: An Official's Killing and the Continued Cartel Push South," STRATFOR, June 17, 2010; and Nick Miroff and William Booth, "Mexican Drug Cartels Bring Violence with Them in Move to Central America," *Washington Post*, July 27, 2010.

[41] "Small Arms Trafficking from the United States to Mexico," 2009, pp. 7–10.

[42] "Small Arms Trafficking from the United States to Mexico," 2009, p. 5; María de la Luz González, "Operación 'hormiga,' en el tráfico de armas," *El Universal*, December 22, 2008.

Table 5.1
General Trafficking Routes, Known Waypoints from U.S.-Mexico Border into Mexico

Route	Entry Points	Onward Destinations
Gulf	Acuna, Piedras Negras, Miguel Alemán, Nuevo Laredo, Reynosa, Matamoros	Chiapas, Veracruz
Pacific	Tijuana, Mexicali, San Luis Río Colorado, Nogales	Sinaloa, Nayarit, Jalisco, Michoacán, Guerrero, Oaxaca
Central	Cuidad Juarez, Piedras Negras	Durango, Jalisco; joins Pacific route
Southern	Balancan, Cuidad Cuauhtemoc, Cuidad Hidalgo	Veracruz, Oaxaca; joins other, unidentified routes

SOURCE: "Small Arms Trafficking from the United States to Mexico," 2009, p. 5. Data reproduced from María González, 2008.

shot in an ambush along with her husband, Arthur Redfels (an officer at the county jail in El Paso), when they were within sight of the Texas border bridge crossing leading back into the United States.[43] Authorities now believe that the executions were ordered and possibly carried out by Eduardo Ravelo, the leader of the Barrio Aztecas—a prison-based gang founded in the mid-1980s that now works for the Juárez cartel.[44]

Problems of cross-border violence have been particularly evident in Arizona. In June 2008, for instance, a group of heavily armed gunmen dressed in the garb of a Phoenix police tactical team fired more than 100 rounds in a targeted killing of a Jamaican cocaine dealer who

---

[43] That same day, assassins killed the partner of another consular employee, triggering fears that Mexican syndicates were engaged in a systematic policy to execute U.S. officials and their families returning to the United States. It now appears that this attack, as well as the murder of Leslie Enriquez, were mistakes, carried out by street gangs who were ordered to kill only Redfels.

[44] Marc Lacey and Ginger Thompson, "Two Drug Slayings in Mexico Rock U.S. Consulate," *New York Times*, March 14, 2010; Marc Lacey, "Raids Aim to Find Killers of 3 in Mexico," *New York Times*, March 18, 2010b.

had double-crossed a Mexican cartel. Heavily armed gunmen have also contributed to the chronic state of kidnapping in Phoenix, which currently remains the worst in the United States.[45] Another state experiencing difficulties is Texas, where merchants and wealthy families in frontier towns periodically face extortion threats from Mexican cartels and where narcotics-related murders are not uncommon. One of the highest-profile killings occurred in September 2008, when the police chief of Ciudad Acuna was assassinated while visiting a friend in Del Rio, Texas.[46]

Besides the weapon trade and its attendant implications for state security, there are now fears that drug-fueled violence could seriously threaten the sovereign writ of a state to the immediate south of the United States. Indeed, according to the U.S. Defense Department, the Sinaloa cartel, Gulf cartel, and Los Zetas can collectively field more than 100,000 foot soldiers, a number that rivals the size of Mexico's standing army of 130,000 troops.[47]

Although not imminent, the possible breakdown of basic civility and law and order in Mexico, and its attendant implications for American security, continues to inform the threat perceptions of Washington. Reflecting this concern was a 2009 assessment by U.S. Joint Forces Command, which candidly remarked,

> [T]he [Mexican] government, its politicians, police and judicial infrastructure are all under sustained assault and pressure by criminal gangs and drug cartels. How that internal conflict turns out over the next several years will have a major impact on the

---

[45] Brian Ross, Richard Esposito, and Asa Eslocker, "Kidnapping Capital of the U.S.A.," *ABC News: The Blotter*, February 11, 2009. The 2008 figure was the highest incidence rate of any city in the world outside Mexico.

[46] See Fred Burton and Scott Stewart, "The Long Arm of the Lawless," *Global Security and Intelligence Report*, February 25, 2009; David Danelo, "Space Invaders: Mexican Illegal Aliens and the US," *Jane's Intelligence Review*, October 29, 2008; Archibold, 2009c; and Sam Quinones, "State of War," *Foreign Policy*, February 16, 2009.

[47] See "100,000 Foot Soldiers in Mexican Cartels," *Washington Times*, March 3, 2009. It should be noted that many commentators believe this figure to be an exaggeration (and one that is largely based on an estimate given by a military official during congressional testimony) and that the actual number is nearer to 10,000.

Table 5.2
Weapons Known to Be Trafficked from the United States to Mexico

Weapon	Model	Manufacturer	Average Price ($) U.S.[a]	Average Price ($) Mexico[b]
0.50-caliber BMG	M82	Barrett	8,000	20,000
AK47	Various	Various	600	1,500
AR-15	Bushmaster	Bushmaster	800	2,000
FN PS90		Fabrique Nationale	1,700	4,250
M-16	Various	Various	750	1,875
M-4 Carbine	Various	Various	800	2,000
0.38 pistol		Colt	600	1,500
0.38 pistol, customized		Colt	10,000	11,000
0.38 caliber "Super"		Colt	1,200	3,000
0.45 caliber pistol		Colt	900	2,250
5.7 mm pistol	Five-Seven Pistol	Fabrique Nationale	1,000	2,500
9 mm handgun	Various	Glock	500	1,250
9 mm handgun	Various	Berretta	550	1,375
Tec-9 semiautomatic handgun		Intratec	500	1,250
M-60		Various	6,000	15,000
Uzi			2,000	6,000
Grenades		Various	Varied	Varied
M-72 rocket		Various	Unknown	Unknown
AT-4 rocket			Unknown	Unknown
RPG-7 launchers			Unknown	Unknown

Table 5.2—Continued

Weapon	Model	Manufacturer	Average Price ($) U.S.[a]	Mexico[b]
37 mm grenade launcher			Unknown	Unknown
40 mm grenade launcher			4,000	10,000
40 mm grenade-launcher rifle attachment			600	1,500
10-gauge shotgun	Various	Various	700	1,750
12-gauge shotgun	Various	Various	450	1,125
High-powered scope			50[c]	125[d]
Silencer			550	1,375

SOURCE: "Small Arms Trafficking from the United States to Mexico," 2009, p. 6. Data compiled from information collated by the National Association of Border Patrol Officers, March 23, 2008.

[a] Prices are derived from an average of the least- and most-expensive weapons listed on GunsAmerica, a nationwide weapon-purchasing website.

[b] In Mexico, most weapon types sell for between two and three times the U.S. market price. For the purposes of this table, the average price in Mexico is therefore assumed to be 2.5 that of the U.S. listing.

[c] With night vision, $400.

[d] With night vision, $1,000.

stability of the Mexican state. Any descent by Mexico into chaos would demand an American response based on the serious implications for homeland security alone.[48]

Mexican narco-groups are also becoming increasingly involved in the U.S. people-smuggling "business." Syndicates often assist migrants

---

[48] Cited in Debusmann, 2009. See also Ryan Christopher DeVault, "Mexico Political Collapse Could Be on Horizon, According to U.S. Joint Forces Report," *Associated Content*, January 14, 2009.

Table 5.3
Popular Weapon Prices, Tucson Gun
Show, March 2009

Weapon	Price ($)
SKS	1,199
0.357 Magnum	549
Uzi (used)	1,700
AK 47 (.762)	950
AR 15 (used)	799[a]
PS90	1,799
M1 Carbine	649

SOURCE: Tucson Gun Show, March 14, 2009.

[a] In cash, $699.

looking to illegally enter the United States on condition that they carry cocaine packs with them.[49] Drug lords have additionally worked with organized human traffickers (known as "coyotes"), allowing them to utilize the same established infrastructure (for a mutually agreed levy) that has been developed to avoid formal custom checkpoints. Notably, this has included access to underground cross-border corridors that run from such cities as Nogales, Tijuana, and Cuidad Juárez.[50] More than 80 cartel-financed subways have been discovered since September 2001, a number of which immigration authorities believe have been used to ferry both people and drugs into the United States. One of the most sophisticated was a passageway that connected a building in Tijuana to

---

[49] See, for instance, National Drug Intelligence Center, 2010, p. 17; U.S. House of Representatives, Committee on Homeland Security Subcommittee on Investigations, majority staff, *A Line in the Sand: Confronting the Threat at the Southwest Border*, undated; Tim Padgett, "People Smugglers Inc.," *Time*, August 12, 2003; Mac Donald, Heather. "The Illegal-Alien Crime Wave," *City Journal*, Winter 2004; and Jameson Taylor, "Illegal Immigration: Drugs, Gangs and Crime," Civitas Institute, November 1, 2007.

[50] Author interviews, Nogales, July 2006. See also National Drug Intelligence Center, 2010, p. 15; "Mexico: Cartels' Danger to the United States," STRATFOR, December 17, 2008; Moore, 2009; and Archibold, 2009b.

a warehouse in San Diego. Known as the La Media tunnel, this subterranean channel was equipped with a concrete floor, ventilation outlets, electric lighting, and a rail-and-cart transportation system.[51]

The Andean drug trade has additionally contributed to a growing problem of Central American gang violence in the United States. Two groups have elicited particular concern.[52] The first is the Mexican La Eme (the Spanish phonetic for the letter "M"), which originally consisted of convicted American-Mexican youths who organized in a Californian prison during the late 1950s. The gang's membership has since expanded to the barrios of eastern Los Angeles, as have its activities, which now embrace extortion, debt collection, and, particularly, drug trafficking. The second is the third-generation (3GEN) El Salvadoran Mara Salvatrucha–13 (MS-13), which was created by Salvadorans fleeing their country's civil war in the 1980s. The organization was initially based in Los Angeles but has since spread to 33 states and retains a particularly strong presence in the "tri-border" region between Washington, D.C., Virginia, and Maryland. Like most other 3GEN organizations, MS-13 operates across a broad spatial spectrum, is characterized by a high degree of structural discipline and sophistication and has developed at least nascent political aims (such as the co-option or weakening of state institutions).[53]

U.S. law enforcement has confirmed that both La Eme and MS-13 are directly involved in the distribution of cocaine and heroin in addition to kidnapping, extortion, auto and people smuggling, and

---

[51] Danelo, 2008.

[52] Apart from these two organizations, several other street gangs have been linked to the distribution of Latin American cocaine in the United States, including Barrio Azteca, Texas Syndicate, and Hermanos Pistoleros.

[53] Jay S. Albanese, "Prison Break: Mexican Gang Moves Operations Outside US Jails," *Jane's Intelligence Review*, December 4, 2008, p. 47; J. Sullivan and Elkus, 2008 p. 4; Adam Elkus, "Gangs, Terrorists, and Trade," *Foreign Policy in Focus*, April 17, 2007; "The World's Most Dangerous Gangs," 2009. For more on 3GEN gangs, see John P. Sullivan, "Maras Morphing: Revisiting Third Generation Gangs," *Global Crime*, Vol. 7, No. 3–4, August–November 2006, pp. 487–504; John P. Sullivan, "Transnational Gangs: The Impact of Third Generation Gangs in Central America," *Air and Space Power Journal*, Second Trimester 2008a.

racketeering.[54] The FBI fears that, as the scope of narcotics trafficking into the country expands, it will attract greater gang involvement (due to the enormous profits that can be garnered from the trade) and, concomitantly, increased violence in an effort to expand local market control.[55] Bureau officials also believe that the intricacies associated with the drug business is necessarily forcing these gangs to systematically transform their hitherto loosely configured structures into ones with a far higher degree of vertical organization.[56] The danger is that this trend will entrench a sustained criminal presence in the heart of mainland America of the sort typically associated with the violence-ridden countries south of the United States.[57] As Sam Logan and Ashley Morse remark,

> Communication between gang members in Central American countries and the leaders of MS-13 [and M-18] factions in Virginia, Maryland, Washington D.C. and other states suggests a trend toward a level of organization normally operated by well established drug smuggling organizations such as the Norte del Valle Cartel in Colombia or Mexico's Sinaloa Federation.[58]

Finally, there are fears of a nexus emerging between Latin American and Mexican narco-groups and Islamist terrorists. One common worry is that jihadists will seek to finance international or antiwestern attacks either by working in tandem with drug cartels or through their

---

[54] It should be noted that there is no concrete evidence of how La Eme or MS-13 actually obtain their drugs. Presumably, consignments are brought in from Mexico, but the precise extent of the links between the gangs themselves and syndicates operating south of the U.S. border remains unclear.

[55] Clare Ribando, *Gangs in Central America*, Washington, D.C.: Congressional Information Service, Library of Congress, 05-RS-22141, May 10, 2005, p. 2. See also Albanese, 2008, pp. 44–47; Moore, 2009; and Burton and Stewart, 2009.

[56] Ribando, 2005, pp. 1–2; Sam Logan and Ashley Morse, "Explosive USA Growth of Central American Gangs," *ISN Security Watch*, January 3, 2007.

[57] An estimated 10–15 percent of Los Angeles' 40,000 gang members are thought to have international ties to Central American organizations. See "Los Angeles, El Salvador Law Enforcement Unite," *Dialogo*, Vol. 19, No. 1, 2009.

[58] Logan and Morse, 2007, p. 2.

own independently generated cocaine profits. There is certainly considerable money to be made through the mark-up sale of the drug. The 2008 wholesale price for a gram of cocaine in Colombia, for instance, was estimated to be around $2.30. That same gram could realistically have been expected to fetch $8.10 in Mexico, $27 in the United States (at average purity levels), $60 in Europe, and as much as $148 in the Russian Federation.[59]

Besides the fact that they offer a source of revenue, officials in Washington have cited two additional concerns: (1) that Middle Eastern, North African, or Asian militants might look to such entities as Los Zetas, the Sinaloa cartel, and Beltrán Leyva Organization to facilitate their covert entry into mainland America, and (2) that the endemic drug-related lawlessness and instability across Mexico's northern border provinces will increasingly encourage extremists to regard this area as a viable forward launching pad for executing attacks inside the United States.[60]

To be sure, there have been periodic claims that Islamist extremists are cooperating with such groups as FARC and helping them smuggle narcotics through Africa to Europe.[61] At the time of this writing, however, there were no credible indications that links of this kind existed. Currently, the only manifestations of what could credibly be called narco-terrorism were FARC's trafficking activities in Colombia (on the assumption that the group has not fully degenerated into a

---

[59] UNODC, 2010, p. 170. See also McDermott, 2010, p. 45; Peter H. Reuter, "The Limits of Supply-Side Drug Control," *Milken Institute Review*, First Quarter 2001, pp. 14–23; Michael Braun, assistant administrator and chief of operations, Drug Enforcement Administration, "Drug Trafficking and Middle Eastern Terrorist Groups: A Growing Nexus?" address to special policy forum, as summarized by Washington Institute rapporteur, Washington, D.C.: Washington Institute for Near East Policy, PolicyWatch 1392, July 25, 2008, p. 27; and Colleen W. Cook, *Mexico's Drug Cartels*, Washington, D.C.: Congressional Research Service, Library of Congress, RL34215, October 16, 2007.

[60] Author interviews, Washington, D.C., January 2009. See also Padgett, 2003, p. 2; and J. Sullivan and Elkus, 2008, p. 9.

[61] See, for instance, Hugh Bronstein, "Colombia Rebels, al Qaeda in 'Unholy' Drug Alliance," Reuters, January 24, 2010.

pure crime entity), SL's continuing involvement with coca protection in Peru, and the 2008 Los Zetas grenade attack in Mexico.[62]

---

[62] Author interviews, Washington, D.C., January 2009. For an overview of past FARC and SL drug-related activities, see Steinitz, 2002.

CHAPTER SIX

U.S. Responses

In moving to mitigate the Latin American cocaine trade and its attendant negative impacts, the United States has focused the bulk of its
attention on (external) supply disruption rather than (internal) demand
reduction. Until at least 2008, the main target of Washington's counternarcotics assistance was Colombia. Over the past ten years, support
has included, among other things, the transfer of ground-based radar
systems, helicopter troop carriers, and various forms of heavy artillery;
the institution of in-country training programs aimed at augment-
ing coastal surveillance and interdiction, port security, containerized
cargo inspections, and high-speed pursuit tactics; the deployment of
U.S. special forces advisers to create elite antidrug units in both the
police and army; and the provision of technical advice and equipment
to facilitate ground and aerial crop-eradication efforts. Most of this
aid has been supplied in the context of Plan Colombia. First launched
by the Pastrana government in 1998 and greatly expanded under the
presidency of Álvaro Uribe with the full backing of the George W.
Bush administration, this broad menu of policy proposals seeks to deal
with all aspects of the country's domestic political, social, economic,
and military ills.[1]

---

[1] The menu of proposals in the original Plan Colombia focused on economic recovery,
financial readjustment measures, strengthening the armed forces, judicial reform, agricul-
tural development, increasing transparency and accountability in local government, improv-
ing the provision of social services, securing peace settlements with FARC and the ELN, and
mitigating the drug trade. See Presidency of the Republic of Colombia, *Plan Colombia: Plan
for Peace, Prosperity and the Strengthening of the State*, Bogota: Office of the President, October 1999 edition. For a detailed and comprehensive economic evaluation of Plan Colombia,

The centerpiece of Plan Colombia, however, is a multifaceted counternarcotics strategy designed to "achieve a 'full court press' on all trafficking organization members and critical nodes to completely disrupt [and] destroy their production and shipping capabilities."[2] Integral to this focus has been a major effort to support the destruction of coca plants. Between 1998 and 2009, the area subjected to manual eradication increased from 3,125 ha to 60,577 ha, while aerial spraying—using a formula known as Roundup® (a mixture of glyphosate and Cosmo-Flux™)—rose by more than 58 percent, from 66,029 ha to 104,772 ha.[3] Between 2003 and 2009, the Bogotá government invested $835 million to underwrite these programs, a figure that is expected to surge to $1.5 billion by 2013.[4]

In line with the deteriorating situation in Mexico, the United States has also started to channel a significant amount of security assistance to the Calderón government.[5] In 2008, the George W. Bush administration passed a supplemental budget bill that included $1.6 billion for a so-called Mérida initiative aimed at combating narcotics trafficking and related crime in Central America. Of this sum, $400 million has been allotted to Mexico alone ($352 million in fiscal year [FY] 2008 and $48 million in FY 2009) and will be used to underwrite equipment, training, and intelligence sharing for counternarcotics, counterterrorism, border security, law enforcement, and general institu-

---

see Daniel Mejia and Pascual Restrepo, *The War on Illegal Drug Production and Trafficking: An Economic Evaluation of Plan Colombia*, Bogota, 2008.

[2]   Cited in Peter Zirnite, "The Militarization of the Drug War in Latin America," *Current History*, Vol. 97, No. 618, 1998, p. 168. See also Michael Shifter, "Colombia at War," *Current History*, Vol. 98, No. 626, 1999, pp. 120–121.

[3]   UNODC, 2010, p. 163; Mejia and Posada, 2008, p. 33.

[4]   Brett Borkan, "Cost of Coca Eradication Skyrockets," *Colombia Reports*, July 1, 2010.

[5]   Prior to 2008, Mexico was not a significant recipient of U.S. security assistance, with typical allocations averaging between $60 million and $70 million per year. For a breakdown of aid packages between 2000 and 2006, see Agnes Gereben Schaefer, Benjamin Bahney, and K. Jack Riley, *Security in Mexico: Implications for U.S. Policy Options*, Santa Monica, Calif.: RAND Corporation, MG-876-RC, 2009, pp. 48–52.

tional building.[6] The first tranche of civil-military aid, amounting to $197 million, was released on December 3, 2008, and will provide

- helicopters and surveillance aircraft to support interdiction and rapid response by Mexican law enforcement agencies
- nonintrusive inspection equipment, ion scanners, and canine units for customs, police, and the military to interdict trafficked drugs, arms, cash, and persons
- technologies and secure communication systems to enhance data collection and storage
- technical advice and training to strengthen judicial institutions and improve vetting for the police; case-management software to track investigations through the legal process; support for offices to oversee citizen complaints and professional responsibility; and assistance in establishing witness-protection programs.[7]

During the 2008 presidential election campaign, Barack Obama specifically supported the Mérida initiative as the logical basis for broadening the scope of cooperation between the United States and Mexico and providing stronger human rights protection than previous aid packages. This commitment was borne out in 2010 with the announcement of an additional US$331 million aid package.[8] The new assis-

---

[6] Robert Munks, "US Releases Anti-Drugs to Mexico," *Jane's Intelligence Review*, January 2009a, p. 4; Luis Rubio, "Mexico: A Failed State?" *Perspectives on the Americas*, February 12, 2009; F. González, 2009, p. 76; Dooley and Medler, 2008; "Securing America's Borders," 2009, pp. 24–25; Alfredo Corchado, "US Military Role Possible in Mexico Drug Fight," *Dallas Morning News*, January 28, 2009.

[7] Schaefer, Bahney, and Riley, 2009, p. 53. For further details on the Mérida initiative, see U.S. Department of State, "The Merida Initiative," fact sheet, June 23, 2009b, and Andrew Selee, *Overview of the Merida Initiative*, Washington, D.C.: Woodrow Wilson International Center for Scholars, May 2008.

[8] It should be noted that Mexico has devoted considerable monies of its own to combat drug-related crime in the country, increasing the defense budget from just $2 billion in 2006 to $9.3 billion in 2009. This investment has been used to mobilize thousands of troops and federal police, underwrite interdiction of drug shipments, implement institutional reform, and enhance inter- and intraagency cooperation and intelligence sharing. See Steve Fainaru and William Booth, "As Mexico Battles Cartels, the Army Becomes the Law," *Washington Post*, April 2, 2009. For more on Mexico's counterdrug strategy, Clare Ribando Seelke,

tance is more civilian-centric in nature and will principally be aimed at strengthening police and judicial institutions, rebuilding communities crippled by poverty and crime, and fostering more-effective intelligence exchanges.[9] A portion of the money will also be used to underwrite experimental programs involving U.S. and Mexican customs and immigration agencies working more closely to coordinate their patrols and deployments in a system of so-called mirrored enforcement. A pilot scheme has already been initiated along an 80-mile stretch of the Arizona/Nogales border and is currently proceeding in line with the military strategy of "gain, maintain and expand."[10]

U.S. efforts to fight the Andean cocaine trade have borne some important results. Thousands of hectares of coca fields have been destroyed as a result of manual-eradication and crop-spraying initiatives.[11] The latter, which falls under the auspices of the Colombian National Police's (CNP's) Anti-Narcotics Directorate (DIRAN), is rated as the most-ambitious such program in the world and is estimated to have been instrumental in preventing 160 MT of cocaine per year from reaching the United States.[12] DIRAN's Heroin Task Force has been equally active in denting poppy cultivation, which, as previously noted, has witnessed a substantial reduction since 2003.[13]

Merida Initiative for Mexico and Central America: Funding and Policy Issues, Washington, D.C.: Congressional Research Service, R40135, April 2010, pp. 20–23; Clare Ribando Seelke and Kristin M. Finklea, *U.S.-Mexican Security Cooperation: The Mérida Initiative and Beyond*, Washington, D.C.: Congressional Research Service, R41349, July 2010; and John Bailey, *Combating Organized Crime and Drug Trafficking in Mexico: What Are U.S. and Mexican Strategies? Are They Working?* San Diego, Calif.: TransBorder Institute, Working Paper Series on U.S.–Mexico Security Cooperation, May 2010, pp. 7–15.

[9] Ginger Thompson and Marc Lacey, "U.S. and Mexico Revise Joint Antidrug Plan," *New York Times*, March 23, 2010.

[10] Preston, 2010.

[11] In 2008, roughly 230,000 hectares of illicit coca crops were destroyed—more than 133,000 through aerial spraying and 96,000 by manual eradication. See U.S. Department of State, *International Narcotics Control Strategy Report*, February 27, 2009a.

[12] "Aerial Eradication," Embassy of the United States, Narcotics Affairs Section, Bogotá, Colombia, undated web page.

[13] U.S. Department of State, 2009a.

Elite police and military drug units have also scored some notable results. DIRAN's Jungle Commandos (Junglas) have been responsible for destroying a significant number of hydrochloride and coca-base laboratories while specialist military Counter-Narcotics Battalion (CNBN) teams have achieved crucial successes in disrupting the senior leadership of FARC.[14] As noted, key eliminations have included Luis Edgar Devia Silva, Manuel Munoz-Ortiz, Alfonso Cano, Gerardo Aguilar, Alexander Farfan, and Jorge Briceño.

Several prominent Mexican drug kingpins have similarly been neutralized, helping to significantly weaken a number of the prominent cartels currently trafficking drugs into the United States. As discussed, this has been particularly apparent with the Tijuana cartel, the Beltrán Leyva Organization, Los Zetas, and El Chiquilín Gang. Equally, the pilot program of parallel border patrols in Nogales appears to be paying dividends, with overall drug-related arrests noticeably down during the first six months of its operation (regarded by both U.S. and Mexican officials as a counterintuitive sign of success).[15]

That said, Washington's overall counternarcotics assistance program has yet to significantly reduce or undermine the Latin American drug trade. Colombia still constitutes the principal source of cocaine for both the U.S. and global markets, accounting for 90 and 80 percent of respective consumption. There is no sign that overall volumes shipped from the country will drop any time soon, with the projected yield for 2009 standing at 54 MT; as noted, if achieved, this would represent the highest output since 2003. Such an outcome might appear counterintuitive given the vast areas of coca leaf that have been destroyed through aerial and manual eradication efforts. However, it is merely indicative of the ease with which crops can be regrown, many of which are capable of surviving in a wide range of climatic conditions. Just as importantly, it is now evident that farmers are planting higher-

---

[14] U.S. Department of State, 2009a.

[15] Preston, 2010.

yield bushes, which means that output can be maintained with smaller acreages.[16]

Indeed, the very use of crop eradication is questionable. As noted above, the projected cost of manual and aerial fumigation programs is expected to surge to $1.5 billion by 2013. The fact that this might not result in any meaningful decline in production obviously calls into question the wisdom of this investment. Crop spraying has also been linked to various adverse health effects. Roundup, for instance, has resulted in fever, eye irritation, gastrointestinal complaints, skin rashes, and dizziness.[17] Moreover, fumigation is essentially an indiscriminate counternarcotics measure in the sense that it can destroy both licit and illicit crops. Taken together, these outcomes can have a highly detrimental impact on popular support for the government, driving local producers into the hands of insurgents and legitimating their rhetoric that the government is engaged in a rapacious drive to destroy peasant livelihoods.[18] Such an outcome could hand FARC a boon of popular support precisely at a time when it is otherwise reeling from critical leadership losses.

There has also been no diminution in drug players operating in Colombia. Although weaker as an insurgent force, FARC remains a prominent and threatening drug-producing and -trafficking entity[19] and could yet benefit from government eradication efforts that inadvertently alienate local farmers; former paramilitaries have reemerged as straight crime syndicates; there are signs that the ELN is increasingly moving into the cocaine business; and at least 350 "baby cartels"

---

[16] Author interview, Bogotá, March 2009. As one U.S. official candidly remarked, "If soybeans could be developed with the same yield as current coca plants, we could solve the world's food crisis."

[17] Mejia and Posada, 2008, p. 33.

[18] See, for instance, Rabasa and Chalk, 2001, p. 66.

[19] Indeed, FARC's involvement in the drug trade is currently greater than ever before. Whereas, in the past, the group primarily focused only on taxing and protecting coca cultivation, today it actively participates in all aspects of the cocaine chain, from the growth of coca leaf to the manufacture of coca base to the production and subsequent trafficking of refined cocaine.

continue to play a significant role in internal distribution and refining activities.

In Mexico, the situation is even worse, with the northern border provinces now in the throes of what amounts to a fully fledged narco-war. This arguably reflects the post-Cali, post-Medellín "Colombian-ization" of the country's drug trade, with increasingly fragmented car-tels engaging each other and the authorities in a highly vicious battle over territory and sales "turf." Moreover, as Schaefer, Bahney, and Riley observe, the Mérida initiative, at least as currently formulated, neither addresses the gap between federal and local police forces nor provides assistance at the municipal level to deal with everyday security issues.[20] Compounding problems is the fact that, of the $1.6 billion appropri-ated by Congress between 2008 and 2010, only 46 percent has been obligated and 9 percent actually disbursed. As a result, many of the programs listed under the aid package are not being fully or effectively implemented.[21]

Finally, trafficking routes from Colombia and the wider Andean region have, by no means, been curtailed, merely shifting in response to extant interdiction approaches. Indeed, the mosaic of smuggling con-duits extending from Latin America is now arguably more complex than ever before, embracing at least five principal "corridors": a Colombia–Caribbean–Mexico route, a Colombia–eastern Pacific–Mexico route, a Peru–Bolivia–Paraguay–Uruguay–Brazil route, a Brazil–Atlantic–Europe route, a Colombia–Venezuela–Atlantic–Europe route, and a Colombia–Venezuela–Atlantic–West Africa–Europe route.

---

[20] Schaefer, Bahney, and Riley, 2009, p. 54.

[21] See Eric L. Olson and Christopher E. Wilson, "GAO Report Finds Merida Initiative Needs Better Performance Measures," San Diego, Calif.: Woodrow Wilson International Center for Scholars, July 2010, p. 2; U.S. Government Accountability Office, *The Mérida Initiative: The United States Has Provided Counternarcotics and Anticrime Support but Needs Better Performance Measures*, Washington D.C., GAO-10-837, July 2010, p. 7. The slow pace of disbursement reflects several bureaucratic shortfalls in the United States, including a lack of staff to administer the program, slow and cumbersome procurement processes, high turn-over among government officials, and delays in negotiations of interagency and bilateral agreements.

CHAPTER SEVEN

Implications and Recommendations for the U.S. Air Force

Although the Latin American drug trade remains primarily a law enforcement issue that is dealt with through various assistance programs run by the departments of State and Justice,[1] managing the problem does have direct implications for the USAF. For Colombia and, increasingly, Mexico, Washington is including antinarcotics support as an integral feature of FID, which is managed by the Pentagon and includes specific provision for the USAF. Critical assistance is channeled through Air Forces Southern (AFSOUTH) as articulated by U.S. Southern Command (USSOUTHCOM) and centers most notably on the provision of Airborne Warning and Control System aircraft (and associated tanker support) to help interdict the flow of drugs shipped from Latin America through the Caribbean and Central American corridors to Mexico and thence to the United States. This is one of USSOUTHCOM's primary missions, which is undertaken in direct collaboration with JIATF-S in Key West. The goals are multipronged and variously aimed at reducing the flow of drugs into the United States, undermining the power of narcotics-trafficking organizations, restoring order and stability in Mexico, and stabilizing the southern U.S. border.[2]

---

[1] Programs run by the Department of State primarily fall under the auspices of the Bureau of International Narcotics and Law Enforcement Affairs (INL). Agencies and initiatives in the Department of Justice relevant to countering the narcotics trade include the International Criminal Investigative Training Assistance Program (ICITAP) and DEA.

[2] Author interview, Key West, March 2009.

In addition, there are several relevant roles that the USAF can and should play in boosting the capacity of Mexico—the geographic epicenter for much of what is occurring in relation to the current cocaine trade—to counter drug production and trafficking. Notably, these include providing reliable aerial monitoring assets; training and equipping crews to fly and maintain these platforms; enhancing intelligence, surveillance, and reconnaissance (ISR) capabilities; and supplying accurate, real-time intelligence (including satellite imagery) to facilitate ground-based and marine interdiction operations.

In undertaking these mission statements, the USAF leadership could usefully draw on the past and present practices that AFSOUTH has had with the central government in Bogotá to develop programs that have low visibility and that can be sustained at a moderate cost. The U.S. experience in Colombia, for instance, has demonstrated the value of relatively inexpensive aerial surveillance and monitoring platforms equipped with a broad array of electronic sensors as a means of quickly and efficiently disseminating actionable intelligence to on-ground rapid-response units.[3]

The key challenge for the USAF will be how to provide enhanced ISR capabilities to the Mexican government, and specifically the armed forces, while respecting and being sensitive to the latter's sense of national sovereignty. Another prominent difficulty will be how to manage and "sell" this assistance at a time when U.S.-Mexico relations are being strained over the issue of border control and associated fears of a "flood" of illegal immigrants and narcotics-related violence being unleashed into the United States. The USAF also has to be alert to the possibility that certain counternarcotics measures could have adverse effects. For instance, anything that decreases the market share for Mexican drug groups could, in fact, increase levels of violence in the country (at least in the short term) by sharpening competition for

---

[3]   Interviews conducted with members of AFSOUTH during 2009 have shown, not surprisingly, that far less priority has been devoted to the Western Hemisphere than to the demands of other theaters. This has, however, generated creative efforts to provide assistance to key allies in the region, such as the Colombian government, through a variety of lower-cost ISR capabilities.

available "sales turf."[4] On the other hand, the rapidly evolving drug crisis provides the USAF leadership with an opportunity to demonstrate its adaptability and institutional responsiveness to a highly complex national security challenge.

Beyond those it is taking in Mexico, there are at least four specific measures that the USAF should consider in looking to further hone and adjust its counternarcotics effort in Latin America:

- Augment aerial surveillance over the Pacific–Central American corridor. This remains the main conduit for transporting illegal Latin American drugs into the United States. Agreements allowing joint aerial patrols with the Colombian air force would be useful (modeled on the accord allowing the United States to detain operators of SPSSs in Colombian waters), as would provision of coastal surveillance assets, such as P-3 Orion aircraft.
- Refine standard operating procedures and further institutionalize joint mission statements and protocols regarding drug interdiction. The USAF might wish to examine ways to work more closely with the U.S. Navy and USCG, particularly in terms of identifying, tracking, and interdicting go-fasts operating up the central American coast, as well as semisubs making drug runs in the eastern Pacific.
- Reconsider the policy of aerial fumigation of crops. Despite the destruction of huge crops in the past, the overall volume of refined cocaine and heroin coming out of Latin America has not declined. Moreover, farmers have adapted by intermingling poppies and coca plants with other crops and by developing plants that are both hardier (capable of growing in adverse environments) and able to produce higher yields. Given the unsatisfactory results of this approach, scarce U.S. resources could be more-usefully spent in such areas as aerial surveillance, capacity building, and demand reduction.

---

[4] The extent to which specific counternarcotics measures complement or contradict one another is an important question and is an area that could usefully be made the subject of future research.

- Ensure adequate protection of existing counternarcotics access agreements in Central America. In addition to the access agreement with Colombia, the United States has signed accords for counterdrug missions with El Salvador and Curacao and has an implied arrangement with Honduras.[5] The pacts in Central America have allowed Washington to establish useful forward bases for monitoring drug shipments in the Caribbean and Pacific. Ensuring that these agreements remain intact has arguably become even more important since 2009, when the USAF base in Manta, Ecuador, was closed.[6] In its interactions with the Department of Defense and other government agencies, the USAF should make protection of these arrangements a main priority and consideration in the formulation of future policy toward Central America.

---

[5]   The accords with El Salvador and Curacao are specific to supporting counterdrug efforts. The protocol with Honduras, however, is more general in nature and allows U.S. basing facilities in Soto Cano to be used for a range of purposes. Whether the forced removal of President Zelaya in 2009 will affect the Honduran agreement remains to be seen.

[6]   John Lindsay-Poland, "Revamping Plan Colombia," *Foreign Policy in Focus*, July 21, 2009; "Last US Forces Abandon Manta Military Base in Ecuador," MercoPress, September 19, 2009.

Bibliography

"69 Are Killed in a Single Day as Mexico Drug War Grinds On," *International Herald Tribune*, January 13, 2010.

"5630 Execution Murders in 2008: Mexican Drug Cartels," *Right Side News*, January 1, 2009.

"100,000 Foot Soldiers in Mexican Cartels," *Washington Times*, March 3, 2009. As of February 9, 2011:
http://www.washingtontimes.com/news/2009/mar/03/100000-foot-soldiers-in-cartels/

Aaron, Christopher, "Coca Production Is on the Increase in Bolivia, Peru," *Jane's Intelligence Review*, January, August 2005.

Abbott, LTC Philip K., U.S. Army, "Terrorist Threat in the Tri-Border Area: Myth or Reality?" *Military Review*, September–October 2004, pp. 51–55. As of February 9, 2011:
http://www.au.af.mil/au/awc/awcgate/milreview/abbott.pdf

"Aerial Eradication," Embassy of the United States, Narcotics Affairs Section, Bogotá, Colombia, undated web page. As of February 9, 2011:
http://bogota.usembassy.gov/nas-eradication.html

Agren, David, "Mexico: Death Toll from Drug-Related Violence Is Thousands Higher Than Was Reported Earlier," *New York Times*, August 3, 2010. As of February 9, 2011:
http://www.nytimes.com/2010/08/04/world/americas/04forbriefs-MEXICO.html

Albanese, Jay S., "Prison Break: Mexican Gang Moves Operations Outside US Jails," *Jane's Intelligence Review*, December 4, 2008.

Álvarez, Ángel, "Capital de Aguascalientes se une a Mando Único Policial," *La Crónica de Hoy*, October 12, 2008. As of February 9, 2011:
http://www.cronica.com.mx/nota.php?id_nota=537390

"America's Most Wanted Drug Smuggler Diego Montoya Caught in Colombia," Associated Press, September 10, 2007.

Archibold, Randal C., "U.S. Plans Border 'Surge' Against Any Drug Wars," *New York Times*, January 7, 2009a. As of February 9, 2011:
http://www.nytimes.com/2009/01/08/us/08chertoff.html

———, "Wave of Drug Violence Is Creeping into Arizona from Mexico, Officials Say," *New York Times*, February 23, 2009b. As of February 11, 2011:
http://www.nytimes.com/2009/02/24/us/24border.html

———, "Drug War in Mexico Pushes into US Homes," *International Herald Tribune*, March 24, 2009c.

———, "U.S. Falters in Screening Border Patrol Near Mexico," *New York Times*, March 11, 2010a. As of February 9, 2011:
http://www.nytimes.com/2010/03/12/us/12border.html

———, "Mexican Leader Pushes Police Overhaul," *New York Times*, October 7, 2010b. As of February 9, 2011:
http://www.nytimes.com/2010/10/08/world/americas/08mexico.html

Bailey, John, *Combating Organized Crime and Drug Trafficking in Mexico: What Are U.S. and Mexican Strategies? Are They Working?* San Diego, Calif.: TransBorder Institute, Working Paper Series on U.S.–Mexico Security Cooperation, May 2010.

Bajak, Frank, "DEA: Seized Submarine Quantum Leap for Narcos," Associated Press, July 4, 2010.

Balko, Radley, "The House of Death," *Reason*, September 30, 2008.

Becerra, Oscar, "A to Z of Crime: Mexico's Zetas Expand Operations," *Jane's Intelligence Review*, January 27, 2009a.

———, "Black Ice: Methamphetamines on the Rise in Mexico," *Jane's Intelligence Review*, September 2009b.

———, "Family Business: La Familia: Mexico's Most Violent Criminals," *Jane's Intelligence Review*, October 7, 2009c.

Berti, Benedetta, "Reassessing the Transnational Terrorism–Criminal Link in South America's Tri-Border Area," *Terrorism Monitor*, Vol. 6, No. 18, September 22, 2008. As of February 9, 2011:
http://www.jamestown.org/programs/gta/
single/?tx_ttnews[tt_news]=5172&tx_ttnews[backPid]=167&no_cache=1

Billeaud, Jacques, "Cartels in Mexico's Drug War Get Guns from US," Associated Press, January 28, 2009.

Binnie, Jeremy, and Christian Le Miere, "In the Line of Fire," *Jane's Intelligence Review*, January 2009.

"Bolivia Expels U.S. Diplomat," Associated Press, March 9, 2009.

Borkan, Brett, "Cost of Coca Eradication Skyrockets," *Colombia Reports*, July 1, 2010. As of February 9, 2011:
http://colombiareports.com/colombia-news/news
/10585-cost-for-new-drug-eradication-program-skyrockets.html

Braun, Michael, assistant administrator and chief of operations, Drug Enforcement Administration, "Drug Trafficking and Middle Eastern Terrorist Groups: A Growing Nexus?" address to special policy forum, as summarized by Washington Institute rapporteur, Washington, D.C.: Washington Institute for Near East Policy, PolicyWatch 1392, July 25, 2008. As of February 9, 2011:
http://www.washingtoninstitute.org/templateC05.php?CID=2914

Brinkley, Joel, "Plan Colombia Is a Failure and Should Be Shut Down," *Plain Dealer Opinion*, March 16, 2009. As of February 9, 2011:
http://blog.cleveland.com/pdopinion/2009/03/
plan_colombia_is_a_failure_and.html

Bronstein, Hugh, "Colombia Rebels, al Qaeda in 'Unholy' Drug Alliance," Reuters, January 24, 2010. As of February 9, 2011:
http://in.reuters.com/article/2010/01/04/idINIndia-45137220100104

Brunelli, Michele, "The Italian Connection: Calabrian Mafia's Power Base Has Expanded," *Jane's Intelligence Review*, December 2008.

Bureau for International Narcotics and Law Enforcement Affairs, "Counternarcotics and Law Enforcement Country Program: Mexico," fact sheet, Washington, D.C.: U.S. Department of State, January 20, 2009. As of February 9, 2011:
http://www.state.gov/p/inl/rls/fs/114078.htm

Burton, Fred, and Stephen Meiners, "Mexico and the War Against the Drug Cartels in 2008," *Global Security and Intelligence Report*, December 9, 2008. As of February 9, 2011:
http://www.stratfor.com/
weekly/20081209_mexico_and_war_against_drug_cartels_2008

Burton, Fred, and Scott Stewart, "The Long Arm of the Lawless," *Global Security and Intelligence Report*, February 25, 2009. As of February 9, 2011:
http://www.stratfor.com/weekly/20090225_long_arm_lawless

Bush, George W., *National Drug Control Strategy 2006 Annual Report*, Washington, D.C., 2006.

―――, *National Drug Control Strategy 2008 Annual Report: Message from the President of the United States Transmitting the Administration's 2008 National Drug Control Strategy, Pursuant to 21 U.S.C. 1504*, Washington, D.C., 2008. As of February 11, 2011:
http://purl.access.gpo.gov/GPO/LPS95337

Central Intelligence Agency, "Mexico," *The World Factbook*, author referenced June 10, 2008. As of February 9, 2011:
https://www.cia.gov/library/publications/the-world-factbook/geos/mx.html

Chalk, Peter, *Non-Military Security and Global Order: The Impact of Extremism, Violence and Chaos on National and International Stability*, London: Macmillan, 2000.

Chaskel, Sebastian, and Michael Bustamante, "Colombia's Precarious Progress," *Current History*, February 2008. As of February 9, 2011:
http://www.cfr.org/content/thinktank/RA%20articles/Chaskel_Bustamante_2_08_Columbia.pdf

"Clinton: U.S. Fueling Mexican Drug Wars," CBS News, March 25, 2009. As of May 20, 2009:
http://www.cbsnews.com/stories/2009/03/25/politics/main4891839.shtml

"The Colombian Cartels," *Frontline Drugwars*, undated. As of February 9, 2011:
http://www.pbs.org/wgbh/pages/frontline/shows/drugs/business/inside/colombian.html

"Colombian FARC Insurgency Could Face Its Most Serious Crisis," Voice of America, July 8, 2008. As of February 10, 2011:
http://www.voanews.com/english/news/a-13-2008-07-08-voa17.html

"Colombian Navy Destroys Drug Sub," *Latin American Herald Tribune*, February 24, 2010. As of February 9, 2011:
http://laht.com/article.asp?CategoryId=12393&ArticleId=352506

Connolly, Ceci, "Woman's Links to Mexican Drug Cartel a Saga of Corruption on U.S. Side of Border," *Washington Post*, September 12, 2010. As of February 11, 2011:
http://www.washingtonpost.com/wp-dyn/content/article/2010/09/11/AR2010091105687.html

Cook, Colleen W., *Mexico's Drug Cartels*, Washington, D.C.: Congressional Research Service, Library of Congress, RL34215, October 16, 2007.

Copeland, Larry, and Kevin Johnson, "Mexican Cartels Plague Atlanta," *USA Today*, March 9, 2009. As of February 11, 2011:
http://www.usatoday.com/news/nation/2009-03-08-mex-cartels_N.htm

Corchado, Alfredo, "Drug Wars' Long Shadow," *Dallas Morning News*, December 13, 2008.

———, "US Military Role Possible in Mexico Drug Fight," *Dallas Morning News*, January 28, 2009.

Danelo, David, "Space Invaders: Mexican Illegal Aliens and the US," *Jane's Intelligence Review*, October 29, 2008.

Daniel, Douglass K., "Gates: US Military Can Help Mexico in Drug Fight," *Associated Press*, March 2, 2009.

Debusmann, Bernard, "Among Top US Fears: A Failed Mexico State," *International Herald Tribune*, January 10, 2009.

DeVault, Ryan Christopher, "Mexico Political Collapse Could Be on Horizon, According to U.S. Joint Forces Report," *Associated Content*, January 14, 2009. As of February 11, 2011:
http://www.associatedcontent.com/article/1388155/
mexico_political_collapse_could_be.html?cat=9

Diaz, Elizabeth, "Analysis: Mexico's Tijuana Cartel Weaker as Ex-Boss Comes Home," Reuters, March 14, 2008.

Dooley, Catherine, and Ariadne Medler, "A Farewell to Arms: Managing Cross-Border Weapons Trafficking," *Hemisphere Focus*, Vol. XVI, No. 2, September 9, 2008. As of February 11, 2011:
http://csis.org/publication/
hemisphere-focus-farewell-arms-managing-cross-border-weapons-trafficking

"Drugs Courier Dies After Swallowing 500g of Cocaine," *Independent* (UK), November 10, 1992.

Elkus, Adam, "Gangs, Terrorists, and Trade," *Foreign Policy in Focus*, April 17, 2007. As of February 11, 2011:
http://www.fpif.org/articles/gangs_terrorists_and_trade

Eller, Andrew, "Mexico's Other Border: Immigration and Drugs Along the Mexican/Guatemala Frontier," *HispanicVista*, undated web page. As of February 11, 2011:
http://www.hispanicvista.com/HVC/Columnist/HVC/Opinion/
Guest_Columns/091010_Andrew_Eller.htm

Ellingwood, Ken, "Extreme Drug Violence Grips Mexico Border City," *Los Angeles Times*, December 19, 2008. As of February 11, 2011:
http://articles.latimes.com/2008/dec/19/world/la-fg-juarezkillings20-2008dec20

———, "Mexican Drug Figure's Son Is Arrested," *Los Angeles Times*, March 20, 2009. As of February 11, 2011:
http://www.latimes.com/news/nationworld/world/
la-fg-mexico-arrest20-2009mar20,0,331303.story

———, "As Mexican Teens Celebrate School Soccer Win, Gunmen Open Fire," *Los Angeles Times*, February 1, 2010. As of February 11, 2011:
http://articles.latimes.com/2010/feb/01/world/la-fg-mexico-shooting1-2010feb01

Emmott, Robin, "Police Corruption Undermines Mexico's War on Drugs," Reuters, May 23, 2007. As of February 11, 2011:
http://www.reuters.com/article/2007/05/23/
us-mexico-drugs-police-idUSN1521094020070523

"Ex–Crime Chief Arrested in Mexico," BBC News, November 21, 2008. As of February 9, 2011:
http://news.bbc.co.uk/2/hi/americas/7742409.stm

Fainaru, Steve, and William Booth, "As Mexico Battles Cartels, the Army Becomes the Law," *Washington Post*, April 2, 2009. As of February 11, 2011:
http://www.washingtonpost.com/wp-dyn/content/article/2009/04/01/AR2009040104335.html

Forero, Juan, "Deep in the Colombian Jungle, Coca Still Thrives," National Public Radio, April 3, 2007. As of February 11, 2011:
http://www.npr.org/templates/story/story.php?storyId=9298685

Freeman, Laurie, *State of Siege: Drug-Related Violence and Corruption in Mexico*, Washington, D.C.: Washington Office on Latin America, June 2006.

Friedman, George, "Mexico: On the Road to a Failed State?" STRATFOR, May 13, 2008. As of February 14, 2011:
http://www.stratfor.com/weekly/mexico_road_failed_state

Garcia, Miguel, "Grenade Attacks Kill 8 on Mexico's National Day," Reuters, September 16, 2008. As of February 11, 2011:
http://www.reuters.com/article/2008/09/17/idUSN16345951

González, Francisco E., "Mexico's Drug Wars Get Brutal," *Current History*, Vol. 108, No. 715, February 2009.

González, María de la Luz, "Operación 'hormiga,' en el tráfico de armas," *El Universal*, December 22, 2008. As of February 11, 2011:
http://www.eluniversal.com.mx/nacion/164626.html

Gonzalez, Mario, "Mexico's Corruption Fight Reaches Civil Workers," *CNN.com*, December 9, 2008. As of February 11, 2011:
http://www.cnn.com/2008/WORLD/americas/12/09/mexico.corruption/index.html

Grayson, George, "Mexico and the Drug Cartels," Foreign Policy Research Institute, August 2007. As of February 11, 2011:
http://www.fpri.org/enotes/200708.grayson.mexicodrugcartels.html

———, "Los Zetas: The Ruthless Army Spawned by a Mexican Drug Cartel," Foreign Policy Research Institute, May 2008. As of February 11, 2011:
http://www.fpri.org/enotes/200805.grayson.loszetas.html

———, "La Familia: Another Deadly Mexican Syndicate," Foreign Policy Research Institute, February 2009. As of February 14, 2011:
http://www.fpri.org/enotes/200901.grayson.lafamilia.html

Guaqueta, Alexandra, "The Colombian Conflict: Political and Economic Dimensions," in Karen Ballentine and Jake Sherman, eds., *The Political Economy of Armed Conflict: Beyond Greed and Grievance*, Boulder, Colo.: Lynne Rienner Publishers, 2003, pp. 73–106.

GunsAmerica, undated home page. As of February 11, 2011:
http://www.gunsamerica.com/

Hanson, Stephanie, "FARC, ELN: Colombia's Left-Wing Guerrillas," Council on Foreign Relations Backgrounder, updated August 19, 2009. As of February 11, 2011:
http://www.cfr.org/colombia/farc-eln-colombias-left-wing-guerrillas/p9272

Harper, Liz, "Colombian Congress Approves Controversial Bill to Revive Peace Talks," *Online News Hour,* June 24, 2005. As of February 11, 2011:
http://www.pbs.org/newshour/updates/colombia_06-24-05.html

"Honduras: An Official's Killing and the Continued Cartel Push South," STRATFOR, June 17, 2010.

Hudson, Rex, *Terrorist and Organized Crime Groups in the Tri-Border Area (TBA) of South America,* Washington, D.C.: Federal Research Division, Library of Congress, July 2003. As of February 11, 2011:
http://handle.dtic.mil/100.2/ADA439846

"In Anti-Drug Move, Mexico Purges Police," *Los Angeles Times,* June 25, 2007.

"In Drug Inquiry, Mexico Arrests Another Top Police Official," Associated Press, November 18, 2008.

International Crisis Group, *War and Drugs in Colombia,* Latin America Report 11, January 2005.

Judd, Terri, "Drug Mule Pensioners: The New Couriers of Choice," *Independent* (UK), December 4, 2008. As of February 11, 2011:
http://www.independent.co.uk/news/uk/crime/
drug-mule-pensioners-the-new-couriers-of-choice-1050593.html

Kenney, Charles, *Fujimori's Coup and the Breakdown of Democracy in Latin America,* Notre Dame, Ind.: University of Notre Dame Press, 2004.

Kilmer, Beau, and Stijn Hoorens, *Understanding Illicit Drug Markets, Supply-Reduction Efforts, and Drug-Related Crime in the European Union,* Santa Monica, Calif.: RAND Corporation, TR-755-EC, 2010. As of February 14, 2011:
http://www.rand.org/pubs/technical_reports/TR755.html

Kilmer, Beau, and Rosalie Liccardo Pacula, *Estimating the Size of the Global Drug Market: A Demand-Side Approach: Report 2,* Santa Monica, Calif.: RAND Corporation, TR-711-EC, 2009. As of February 11, 2011:
http://www.rand.org/pubs/technical_reports/TR711.html

Kirschke, Joseph, "The Coke Coast: Cocaine's New Venezuelan Address," *World Politics Review,* September 11, 2008. As of February 11, 2011:
http://www.worldpoliticsreview.com/articles/2631/
the-coke-coast-cocaines-new-venezuelan-address

Kraul, Chris, "Colombian Drug Lord Killed," *Los Angeles Times*, February 2, 2008a. As of February 11, 2011:
http://articles.latimes.com/2008/feb/02/world/fg-narco2

———, "New Gangs Run Colombians Off Their Land," *Los Angeles Times*, December 3, 2008b. As of February 11, 2011:
http://articles.latimes.com/2008/dec/03/world/fg-paras3

———, "Paramilitary Groups Still Spread Terror Among Colombia's People," *Los Angeles Times*, December 5, 2008c.

———, "DEA Presence Ends in Bolivia," *Los Angeles Times*, January 30, 2009a. As of February 11, 2011:
http://articles.latimes.com/2009/jan/30/world/fg-bolivia-dea30

———, "Colombia Police Arrest Major Drug Figure," *Los Angeles Times*, April 16, 2009b. As of February 11, 2011:
http://articles.latimes.com/2009/apr/16/world/fg-colombia-drugbust16

Lacey, Marc, "Blasts Kill 7 at Celebration in Mexican President's Hometown," *New York Times*, September 16, 2008a. As of February 11, 2011:
http://www.nytimes.com/2008/09/17/world/americas/17mexico.html

———, "Officials Say Drug Cartels Infiltrated Mexican Law Unit," *New York Times*, October 27, 2008b. As of February 11, 2011:
http://www.nytimes.com/2008/10/28/world/americas/28mexico.html

———, "Mexican Man Admits Using Acid on Bodies, Army Says," *New York Times*, January 24, 2009a. As of February 11, 2011:
http://www.nytimes.com/2009/01/25/world/americas/25mexico.html

———, "With Force Mexican Drug Cartels Get Their Way," *New York Times*, February 28, 2009b. As of February 11, 2011:
http://www.nytimes.com/2009/03/01/world/americas/01juarez.html?_r=1

———, "Top Mexican Drug Suspect Arrested," *International Herald Tribune*, January 14, 2010a.

———, "Raids Aim to Find Killers of 3 in Mexico," *New York Times*, March 18, 2010b.

Lacey, Marc, and Ginger Thompson, "Two Drug Slayings in Mexico Rock U.S. Consulate," *New York Times*, March 14, 2010.

LaFranchi, Howard, "A Look Inside a Giant Drug Cartel," *Christian Science Monitor*, December 6, 1999. As of February 11, 2011:
http://www.csmonitor.com/1999/1206/p1s1.html

"Last US Forces Abandon Manta Military Base in Ecuador," MercoPress, September 19, 2009. As of February 9, 2011:
http://en.mercopress.com/2009/09/19/
last-us-forces-abandon-manta-military-base-in-ecuador

Le Miere, Christian, "Insurgent Submersibles," *Jane's Terrorism and Security Monitor*, June 16, 2008.

Leinwand, Donna, "Authorities Try to Keep Guns from Drug Cartels," *USA Today*, December 10, 2008. As of February 11, 2011:
http://www.usatoday.com/news/world/2008-12-10-drugwar_N.htm

Levitt, Matthew, and Michael Jacobson, "Drug Wars," *New Republic*, January 27, 2009. As of February 11, 2011:
http://www.washingtoninstitute.org/templateC06.php?CID=1223

Lindsay-Poland, John, "Revamping Plan Colombia," *Foreign Policy in Focus*, July 21, 2009. As of February 11, 2011:
http://www.fpif.org/articles/revamping_plan_colombia

Llana, Sara Miller, "Setbacks in Mexico's War on Corruption," *Christian Science Monitor*, December 30, 2008. As of February 11, 2011:
http://www.csmonitor.com/World/Americas/2008/1230/p06s02-woam.html

Logan, Sam, "Parallel Governance and Criminal Insurgency in Mexico," paper presented to the RAND Insurgency Board Meeting, Arlington, Va., January 28, 2010.

Logan, Sam, and Ashley Morse, "Explosive USA Growth of Central American Gangs," *ISN Security Watch*, January 3, 2007.

"Los Angeles, El Salvador Law Enforcement Unite," *Dialogo*, Vol. 19, No. 1, 2009.

Lujan, Fernando M., "The Enemy Next Door: Hezbollah in South America," *Roguely Stated*, May 31, 2007. As of February 11, 2011:
http://www.roguelystated.com/2007/05/31/
the-enemy-next-door-hezbollah-in-south-america/

Mac Donald, Heather. "The Illegal-Alien Crime Wave," *City Journal*, Winter 2004. As of February 11, 2011:
http://www.city-journal.org/html/14_1_the_illegal_alien.html

Malkin, Elisabeth, "Mexico Arrests Ex-Chief of Antidrug Agency," *New York Times*, November 21, 2008.

Marosi, Richard, "A City Goes Silent at His Name," *Los Angeles Times*, December 18, 2008. As of February 11, 2011:
http://articles.latimes.com/2008/dec/18/world/fg-tijuanadruglord18

Marosi, Richard, and Ken Ellingwood, "Mexican Drug Lord Teodoro Garcia Simental, Known for His Savagery, Is Captured," *Los Angeles Times*, January 13, 2010. As of February 11, 2011:
http://articles.latimes.com/2010/jan/13/world/la-fg-mexico-arrest13-2010jan13

Matrix Knowledge Group, *The Illicit Drug Trade in the United Kingdom*, London: Home Office, 2007.

McDermott, Jerry, "Colombia Reports Death of FARC Leader," *Daily Telegraph* (UK), May 27, 2008.

———, "Generational Shift: Colombia's Evolving Drug Cartel," *Jane's Intelligence Review*, February 2010.

McDougall, Alex, "State Power and Its Implications for Civil War in Colombia," *Studies in Conflict and Terrorism*, Vol. 32, No. 4, April 2009, pp. 322–345.

McKinley, James C., "Gunmen Kill Chief of Mexico's Police," *New York Times*, May 9, 2008a.

———, "6 Charged in Shooting of Officer in Mexico," *New York Times*, May 13, 2008b.

———, "Two Sides of a Border: One Violent, One Peaceful," *New York Times*, January 22, 2009.

Mejia, Daniel, and Carlos Esteban Posada, *Cocaine Production and Trafficking: What Do We Know?* Washington, D.C.: World Bank Policy Research Working Paper 4618, May 1, 2008.

Mejia, Daniel, and Pascual Restrepo, *The War on Illegal Drug Production and Trafficking: An Economic Evaluation of Plan Colombia*, Bogota, 2008.

"Mexican Army Captures Alleged Leader of Drug Cartel Assassins," Associated Press, January 23, 2008.

"Mexican Drug Lord Is Arrested," Reuters, October 26, 2008.

"Mexico Arrests 2 Reputed Leaders of Tijuana Gang," Associated Press, February 8, 2010.

"Mexico Captures Brother of Slain Cartel Boss," Associated Press, January 3, 2010.

"Mexico: Cartels' Danger to the United States," STRATFOR, December 17, 2008. As of February 9, 2011:
http://www.stratfor.com/analysis/20081217_mexico_cartels_danger_united_states

"Mexico: Cocaine Found in Small Sub," Reuters, July 19, 2008.

"Mexico Corruption, U.S. Weapons Deepen Drug War Toll," *newsdesk.org*, April 5, 2007. As of February 9, 2011:
http://newsdesk.org/2007/04/mexico_corrupti/

"Mexico Town's Entire Police Force Quits in Fear of Assassination," Associated Press, May 23, 2008.

"Mexico's Attorney General Calls on US to Stop Guns, Drug Money," Associated Press, March 29, 2007.

"Mexico's Drug Wars," *Financial Times* (UK), November 26, 2008.

"Mexico's Gun Laws for Americans," *Panda Programming*, last updated June 2, 2010. As of July 29, 2010:
http://www.panda.com/mexicoguns/

Meyer, Josh, "48 Arrested in U.S. Raid on Mexican Drug Cartel," *Los Angeles Times*, February 26, 2009. As of February 11, 2011:
http://articles.latimes.com/2009/feb/26/nation/na-mexico-drug-cartel26

Ministry of National Defense, "The FARC at their Worst Moment in History," September 15, 2008.

Miroff, Nick, and William Booth, "Mexican Drug Cartels Bring Violence with Them in Move to Central America," *Washington Post*, July 27, 2010. As of February 11, 2011:
http://www.washingtonpost.com/wp-dyn/content/article/2010/07/26/AR2010072605661.html

Moore, Solomon, "Tougher Border Can't Stop Mexican Marijuana Cartels," *New York Times*, February 1, 2009.

Munks, Robert, "US Releases Anti-Drugs to Mexico," *Jane's Intelligence Review*, January 2009a.

———, "Brazilian Police Officers Storm the Favelas," *Jane's Intelligence Review*, February 2009b.

———, "Mexico Murders Presage More Violence," *Jane's Intelligence Review*, February 2010.

"Narco Subs: New Challenge in the Drug War," *Dialogo*, Vol. 18, No. 4, 2008.

National Drug Intelligence Center, *National Drug Threat Assessment 2010*, Washington, D.C., February 2010. As of February 11, 2011:
http://www.justice.gov/ndic/pubs38/38661/38661p.pdf

"National Section," *La Reforma*, January 6, 2009.

Nelson, Lauren, "Obama on Latin America," Council on Hemispheric Affairs, October 16, 2008. As of February 11, 2011:
http://www.coha.org/obama-on-latin-america/

"Norte del Valle Cartel Is Finished: Naranjo," *Colombia Reports*, December 12, 2008. As of February 9, 2011:
http://colombiareports.com/colombia-news/news/2310-norte-del-valle-cartel-is-finished-naranjo.html

"Not Winning the War on Drugs," *New York Times*, July 2, 2008.

Office of National Drug Control Policy, *The President's National Drug Control Policy*, Washington, D.C., January 2009. As of February 11, 2011:
http://www.whitehousedrugpolicy.gov/publications/policy/ndcs09/index.html

Olson, Eric L., and Christopher E. Wilson, "GAO Report Finds Merida Initiative Needs Better Performance Measures," San Diego, Calif.: Woodrow Wilson International Center for Scholars, July 2010. As of October 15, 2010: http://www.wilsoncenter.org/topics/docs/ GAO%20Merida%20Initiative%20Report%20Analysis%207.22.pdf

"Organized Crime in Mexico," STRATFOR, March 11, 2008. As of February 14, 2011: http://www.stratfor.com/analysis/organized_crime_mexico

Padgett, Tim, "People Smugglers Inc.," *Time*, August 12, 2003. As of February 11, 2011: http://www.time.com/time/magazine/article/0,9171,474582,00.html

Palmer, David Scott, ed., *The Shining Path of Peru*, New York: St. Martin's Press, 2nd ed., 1994.

Porch, Douglas, and María José Rasmussen, "Demobilization of Paramilitaries in Colombia: Transformation or Transition?" *Studies in Conflict and Terrorism*, Vol. 31, No. 6, June 2008, pp. 520–540.

Presidency of the Republic of Colombia, *Plan Colombia: Plan for Peace, Prosperity and the Strengthening of the State*, Bogota: Office of the President, October 1999 edition.

Preston, Julia, "Officers Team Up to Quell Violence," *New York Times*, March 26, 2010.

Quinones, Sam, "State of War," *Foreign Policy*, February 16, 2009. As of February 11, 2011: http://www.foreignpolicy.com/articles/2009/02/16/state_of_war

Rabasa, Angel, and Peter Chalk, *Colombian Labyrinth: The Synergy of Drugs and Insurgency and Its Implications for Regional Stability*, Santa Monica, Calif.: RAND Corporation, MR-1339-AF, 2001. As of February 11, 2011: http://www.rand.org/pubs/monograph_reports/MR1339.html

Reuter, Peter H., "The Limits of Supply-Side Drug Control," *Milken Institute Review*, First Quarter 2001, pp. 14–23. As of February 11, 2011: http://www.rand.org/pubs/reprints/RP942.html

Reuter, Peter H., and Victoria A. Greenfield, "Measuring Global Drug Markets: How Good Are the Numbers and Why Should We Care About Them?" *World Economics*, Vol. 2, No. 4, October–December 2001, pp. 159–173. As of February 14, 2011: http://www.rand.org/pubs/reprints/RP999.html

Ribando, Clare, *Gangs in Central America*, Washington, D.C.: Congressional Information Service, Library of Congress, 05-RS-22141, May 10, 2005.

Richani, Nazih, *Systems of Violence: The Political Economy of War and Peace in Colombia*, Albany, N.Y.: State University of New York Press, 2002.

"Riverine Operations Set Sights on Drug Traffickers," *Dialogo*, Vol. 18, No. 4, 2008.

Roig-Franzia, Manuel, "U.S. Guns Behind Cartel Killings in Mexico," *Washington Post*, October 29, 2007. As of February 11, 2011:
http://www.washingtonpost.com/wp-dyn/content/article/2007/10/28/AR2007102801654.html

Romero, Mauricio, "Changing Identities and Contested Settings: Regional Elites and the Paramilitaries in Colombia," *International Journal of Politics, Culture and Society*, Vol. 14, No. 1, 2000, pp. 51–69.

Romero, Simon, "Settling of Crisis Makes Winners of Andes Nations, While Rebels Lose Ground," *New York Times*, March 9, 2008.

———, "Cocaine Trade Helps Rebels Reignite War in Peru," *New York Times*, March 17, 2009a.

———, "Wider Drug War Threatens Colombian Indians," *New York Times*, April 21, 2009b.

———, "Coca Production Makes a Comeback in Peru," *New York Times*, June 13, 2010a.

———, "Rebels' Second in Command Has Been Killed, Colombia Says," *New York Times*, September 23, 2010b.

Rose, David, "House of Death," *Observer* (UK), December 3, 2006. As of February 11, 2011:
http://www.guardian.co.uk/world/2006/dec/03/usa.davidrose

Ross, Brian, Richard Esposito, and Asa Eslocker, "Kidnapping Capital of the U.S.A.," *ABC News: The Blotter*, February 11, 2009. As of February 11, 2011:
http://abcnews.go.com/Blotter/story?id=6848672&page=1

Rozema, Ralph, "Urban DDR-Processes: Paramilitaries and Criminal Networks in Medellín, Colombia," *Journal of Latin American Studies*, Vol. 40, No. 3, 2008, pp. 423–452.

Rubio, Luis, "Mexico: A Failed State?" *Perspectives on the Americas*, February 12, 2009.

Saab, Bilal Y., and Alexandra W. Taylor, "Criminality and Armed Groups: A Comparative Study of FARC and Paramilitary Groups in Colombia," *Studies in Conflict and Terrorism*, Vol. 32, No. 6, June 2009, pp. 455–475.

Sabet, Daniel, *Police Reform in Mexico: Advances and Persistent Obstacles*, Wilson Center, undated. As of February 11, 2011:
http://www.wilsoncenter.org/topics/pubs/Sabet.pdf

Schaefer, Agnes Gereben, Benjamin Bahney, and K. Jack Riley, *Security in Mexico: Implications for U.S. Policy Options*, Santa Monica, Calif.: RAND Corporation, MG-876-RC, 2009. As of February 11, 2011:
http://www.rand.org/pubs/monographs/MG876.html

Schoofs, Mark, and Paulo Prada, "Cocaine Boom in Europe Fuels New Laundering Tactics," *Wall Street Journal*, January 16, 2008. As of February 11, 2011:
http://online.wsj.com/article/SB120044304824892769.html

"Securing America's Borders," *Jane's Homeland Security Review*, February 2009.

Seelke, Clare Ribando, *Merida Initiative for Mexico and Central America: Funding and Policy Issues*, Washington, D.C.: Congressional Research Service, R40135, April 2010.

Seelke, Clare Ribando, and Kristin M. Finklea, *U.S.-Mexican Security Cooperation: The Mérida Initiative and Beyond*, Washington, D.C.: Congressional Research Service, R41349, July 2010.

Selee, Andrew, *Overview of the Merida Initiative*, Washington, D.C.: Woodrow Wilson International Center for Scholars, May 2008. As of February 14, 2011:
http://www.wilsoncenter.org/news/docs/
Analysis.Merida%20Initiative%20May%208%202008.pdf

Serrano, Alfonso, "U.S.-Bought Guns Killing Mexican Police," CBS News, August 16, 2007. As of February 9, 2011:
http://www.cbsnews.com/stories/2007/08/16/world/main3174091.shtml

Shifter, Michael, "Colombia at War," *Current History*, Vol. 98, No. 626, 1999.

"Small Arms Trafficking from the United States to Mexico," *Universal Adversary Special Analysis*, February 1, 2009.

Steinitz, Mark S., "The Terrorism and Drug Connection in Latin America's Andean Region," *Policy Papers on the Americas*, Vol. XIII, Study 5, July 2002. As of August 9, 2010:
http://www.revistainterforum.com/english/pdf_en/pp_steinitz.pdf

Steller, Tim, "Mexican Drug Runners May Have Used C-130 from Arizona," *Arizona Daily Star*, April 15, 1998.

Stern, Steve J., ed., *Shining and Other Paths: War and Society in Peru, 1980–1995*, Durham, N.C.: Duke University Press, 1998.

Sullivan, John P., "Maras Morphing: Revisiting Third Generation Gangs," *Global Crime*, Vol. 7, No. 3–4, August–November 2006, pp. 487–504.

———, "Transnational Gangs: The Impact of Third Generation Gangs in Central America," *Air and Space Power Journal*, Second Trimester 2008a. As of February 14, 2011:
http://www.airpower.maxwell.af.mil/apjinternational/apj-s/2008/2tri08/sullivaneng.htm

———, "Outside View: Mexico's Criminal Insurgency," United Press International, December 18, 2008b.

Sullivan, John P., and Adam Elkus, "State of Siege: Mexico's Criminal Insurgency," *Small Wars Journal*, August 2008. As of August 9, 2010:
http://www.smallwarsjournal.com/mag/docs-temp/84-sullivan.pdf

Sullivan, Mark P., *Latin America: Terrorism Issues*, Washington, D.C.: Congressional Information Service, Library of Congress, 06-RS-21049b, January 18, 2006.

Taylor, Jameson, "Illegal Immigration: Drugs, Gangs and Crime," Civitas Institute, November 1, 2007. As of February 14, 2011:
http://www.nccivitas.org/2007/illegal-immigration-drugs-gangs-and-crime/

Thompson, Ginger, and Marc Lacey, "U.S. and Mexico Revise Joint Antidrug Plan," *New York Times*, March 23, 2010.

Trans-Border Institute, "Border Resources," undated web page. As of February 14, 2011:
http://www.sandiego.edu/peacestudies/tbi/resources/

Tuckman, Jo, "Body Count Mounts as Drug Cartels Battle Each Other—and the Police," *Guardian* (UK), May 27, 2008a. As of February 14, 2011:
http://www.guardian.co.uk/world/2008/may/27/mexico

———, "Revellers Killed in Grenade Attack on Mexican Independence Celebrations," *Guardian* (UK), September 16, 2008b. As of February 14, 2011:
http://www.guardian.co.uk/world/2008/sep/16/mexico.drugstrade

———, "Hillary Clinton Admits US Role in Mexico Drug Wars," *Guardian* (UK), March 26, 2009. As of February 14, 2011:
http://www.guardian.co.uk/world/2009/mar/26/mexico-hillary-clinton-drugs-weapons

United Nations High Commissioner for Refugees, "Freedom in the World 2008: Dominican Republic," *Refworld*, July 2, 2008.

United Nations Office on Drugs and Crime, *World Drug Report 2007*, 2007a. As of February 14, 2011:
http://www.unodc.org/unodc/en/data-and-analysis/WDR-2007.html

———, *Coca Cultivation in the Andean Region: A Survey of Bolivia, Colombia, Ecuador and Peru*, June 2007b. As of February 14, 2011:
http://www.unodc.org/documents/crop-monitoring/Andean_report_2007.pdf

————, *World Drug Report 2008*, 2008. As of February 14, 2011:
http://www.unodc.org/unodc/en/data-and-analysis/WDR-2008.html

————, *World Drug Report 2010*, 2010.

U.S. Department of State, *International Narcotics Control Strategy Report*, Washington, D.C., 2007. As of February 14, 2011:
http://www.state.gov/p/inl/rls/nrcrpt/2007/index.htm

————, *International Narcotics Control Strategy Report*, February 27, 2009a. As of February 15, 2011:
http://www.state.gov/p/inl/rls/nrcrpt/2009/index.htm

————, "The Merida Initiative," fact sheet, June 23, 2009b. As of July 29, 2010:
http://www.state.gov/p/inl/rls/fs/122397.htm

————, *International Narcotics Control Strategy Report*, March 2010. As of February 14, 2011:
http://www.state.gov/p/inl/rls/nrcrpt/2010/index.htm

————, *International Narcotics Control Strategy Report*, March 2011. As of March 31, 2011:
http://www.state.gov/p/inl/rls/nrcrpt/2011/vol1

U.S. Government Accountability Office, *The Mérida Initiative: The United States Has Provided Counternarcotics and Anticrime Support but Needs Better Performance Measures*, Washington D.C., GAO-10-837, July 2010. As of February 11, 2011:
http://www.gao.gov/products/GAO-10-837

U.S. House of Representatives, Committee on Homeland Security Subcommittee on Investigations, majority staff, *A Line in the Sand: Confronting the Threat at the Southwest Border*, undated. As of February 11, 2011:
http://www.house.gov/sites/members/tx10_mccaul/pdf/
Investigaions-Border-Report.pdf

Verini, James, "Arming the Drug Wars," *Portfolio*, June 16, 2008. As of February 14, 2011:
http://www.portfolio.com/news-markets/international-news/portfolio/2008/06/16/
Examining-the-US-Mexico-Gun-Trade/

Walsh, John, senior associate, Washington Office on Latin America, "U.S. Drug Policy: At What Cost? Moving Beyond the Self-Defeating Supply-Control Fixation," statement at "Illegal Drugs: Economic Impact, Societal Costs, Policy Responses," hearing of the U.S. Congress Joint Economic Committee, June 19, 2008. As of February 9, 2011:
http://jec.senate.gov/
public/?a=Files.Serve&File_id=745af217-b72f-4b0e-b596-30d171d03cbb

Webb-Vidal, Andy, "Fight the Future," *Jane's Intelligence Review*, September 2008.

————, "Cocaine Coasts: Venezuela and West Africa's Drug Axis," *Jane's Intelligence Review*, February 2009a.

———, "Secret Weapon," *Jane's Intelligence Review*, April 2009b.

———, "Back from the Dead," *Jane's Intelligence Review*, May 2009c.

Wessely, Joe, "Peru: Former Spy Chief Vladimiro Montesinos Gets 20-Year Sentence for Arms Sale to Colombian Rebels," *Latin America Data Base*, Latin American and Iberian Institute, University of New Mexico, October 6, 2006.

Wilkinson, Tracy, "U.S. War on Drugs Has Failed, Report Says," *Los Angeles Times*, November 27, 2008. As of February 14, 2011:
http://www.latimes.com/news/nationworld/world/
la-fg-mexdrugs27-2008nov27,0,7441414.story

———, "Mexico Drug Bosses May Have Set Truce," *Los Angeles Times*, January 29, 2009. As of February 14, 2011:
http://www.latimes.com/news/nationworld/world/latinamerica/
la-fg-narco-truce29-2009jan29,0,5459015.story

"The World's Most Dangerous Gangs," *Dialogo*, Vol. 19, No. 1, 2009.

Zirnite, Peter, "The Militarization of the Drug War in Latin America," *Current History*, Vol. 97, No. 618, 1998.